COPYRIGHT IN FURTHER AND HIGHER EDUCATION LIBRARIES

Third edition

REVISED AND UPDATED BY

Sandy Norman

Library Association Publishing
London

Acknowledgements

I gratefully acknowledge the contributions from Denis Heathcote, Librarian of the University of Greenwich and the SCONUL representative on the LA/JCC Working Party on Copyright; David List especially for his knowledge of photographs; the help and guidance from Philip Plumb, the Chair of the Working Party; as well as the hundreds of other LA members from the further and higher education sector who, over the past seven years, have presented me with a variety of copyright problems to solve.

Further advice

Library Association members who need further information on copyright matters are advised to contact LAHQ in the first instance. Please contact Sandy Norman, Information Manager (Legal and Parliamentary), Information Services. Tel: 0171 636 7543; Fax: 0171 436 7218; e-mail: sandy@la-hq.org.uk.

Disclaimer

Whilst every care has been taken in compiling these notes, The Library Association, in the absence of clear definitions in the legislation and of court decisions, and in the light of differences of opinion between experts in copyright law, cannot claim that they are definitive nor do they constitute legal advice. If in doubt, it is advised to err on the side of caution and, where necessary, to seek appropriate legal advice.

This edition entirely supersedes *Copyright in polytechnic and university libraries* published by the LA in October 1990.

British Library Cataloguing in Publication Data
A catalogue record for this book is available from the British Library

ISBN 1-85604-196-4

Typeset from author's disk in Aldine 721 and Arial by Library Association Publishing
Printed and made in Great Britain by Amber (Printwork) Ltd, Harpenden, Herts.

Contents

Preface to the third edition 5

Introduction 5

Copyright: the main provisions of the Act 6
What is copyright? 6
Materials subject to copyright 6
Length of the copyright period 6
  Literary, dramatic, musical or artistic works 6
  Films 6
  Sound recordings, broadcasts, cable programmes and computer generated works 6
  Typographical arrangements of published works 6
Who owns the copyright? 6
Copyright restrictions 7
What is copyright infringement? 7
Secondary infringement [SS.22–26] 7
Moral rights 7
Penalties 7

Exceptions to exclusive rights 8
Fair dealing 8
  Fair dealing: research or private study [S.29] 8
  Fair dealing: criticism or review [S.30(1)] 8
  Fair dealing: news reporting [S30(2)] 8
  Incidental inclusion [S.31] 8
Copying by librarians and archivists 9
  Copying service (local or interlibrary document supply) [SS.38–40] 9
  Interlibrary copying for stock [S.41] 9
  Copying for replacement [S.42] 10
  Copying unpublished works [S.43] 10
Special rules for education [S.32–35] 10
  Copying for instruction [S.32] 10
  Copying for examinations [S.32(3)] 10
  Performing a literary, dramatic or musical work [S.34] 10
  Off-air recording [S.35] 10
  Copying audiovisual material for teaching film and sound recording production [S.32(3)] 10

Other exceptions and permissions 11
Abstracts [S.60] 11
Advertising art works for sale [S.63] 11
Anonymous works [S.57] 11
Free public showing or playing of a broadcast or cable programme [S.72] 11
Off-air recording [S.70] 11
Parliamentary and judicial proceedings [S.45] 11
Photograph of a television broadcast or cable programme [S.71] 11
Playing of sound recordings in clubs [S.67] 11
Provision of subtitled copies of broadcast and cable programmes [S.74] 11
Public inspection [S.47] 11
Reading in public [S.59] 11
Royal Commission or statutory enquiry [S.46] 11

Guidance on copying limits 11
Number of copies 11
Published literary works 11
  Periodicals 11
  Books 12
  Short books, reports or pamphlets without chapters 12
  Poems, short stories and other short literary works 12
  British Standards 12
  Crown and Parliamentary publications including HMSO material 12
  Official Journal of the EU 13
  Yellow Pages 13
Artistic works 13
  Illustrations 13
  Ordnance Survey maps 13
  Goad plans 13
  Photographs 13
  Slides or transparencies 13
Music 14

Licensing 14
Copyright Licensing Agency licensing schemes 14
  Further education licence 14
  Higher education licence 14
  BL/CLA agreement 15
DACS slide licensing scheme 15
Off-air recording licensing schemes 15
  ERA licence 15
  OUEE licence 16
Other licencing schemes 16
  UK pilot site licence initiative 16
  Ordnance Survey education licences 16
  British Standards Institution licence 16
  Newspaper Licensing Agency 16

Rental and lending 16

EU Directives 16
Computer software 17
Extension of the term of protection 17
Rental and Lending Directive 17
Legal protection of databases 17
Other EU Directives 18

Electronic copyright 18
Electrocopying 18
    Electrocopying guidelines 19

Miscellaneous advice and guidance 20
Charging for copying 20
Committee papers 20
Contents pages 21
Copyright cleared work books 21
Copying artistic works as part of a slide catalogue 21
Copying by students in public libraries 22
Copying for stock 22
Copying for the visually impaired 22
Copying from newspapers 22
Current awareness bulletins 22
Damaged tapes 23
Declaration forms 23
Exhibitions 23
Foreign material 23
Free material 23
Market research reports 23
Microforms 23
Mixed media packages 23
Permission 23
Photographs 23
Playing music in educational establishments 24
Profit basis 24
Prohibitive statements 24
Self-service photocopiers and liability 24
Short loan and reserve collections 25
Theses and dissertations 25
Translations 25
Unpublished works 25
Videos 25
Whole works 26
Works created under the terms of an employment
    contract 26

Case law 26
Artistic works 26
Artistic works: maps 26
Artistic works: photographs 26
Books and periodicals 26
Computer software 27
Music 27
Videos 27
Performance right 28
Rental right 28
Electronic copyright 28

Posters 28

Other LA guides 28

LA/JCC Working Party on Copyright 28

Appendix A: Prescribed libraries and archives 29

Appendix B: Prescribed copyright declaration form 30

Appendix C: List of useful addresses 31

The Act and relevant Statutory Instruments 32

Further reading list 32

Index 33

Preface to the third edition

The main aims of this work are to promote respect and understanding of copyright and to help library and information staff continue to provide a good service to their clientele whilst remaining on the right side of the law. Since the publication of the previous editions of these LA sectoral guides, there have been many new developments in the area of copyright and neighbouring rights: European Union legislation; advances in technology and telecommunications; and various licensing and voluntary agreements. A third edition is now long overdue.

The format of this guide is similar to the previous edition. Much of the information contained in the sections on the **Main provisions of the Act** and the **Exceptions to exclusive rights** is the same as in the second edition but has been reorganized in the interests of clarity. There is a new section on **Moral rights** and a selection of relevant **Case law** has been included. The section on audiovisual and electronic copyright has been completely revised to take into account the amendments to the Act, EU Directives and electrocopying issues. The **Miscellaneous advice and guidance** section has been updated, expanded and reorganized.

Introduction

These guidelines are intended primarily for librarians and information professionals working in further and higher education establishments. They can also be a useful source of copyright information and guidance on copyright and licensing issues for teachers, technicians, reprographics staff, researchers and other members of universities, institutions of higher education and FE colleges. The purpose of the guidelines is to provide an easy to understand insight into copyright law from the point of view of the information intermediary and the users of information.

They can be read by those having limited or even no knowledge of copyright and wishing to learn, and those who deal with copyright issues daily and who wish to keep themselves up to date.

There are separate copyright guides available for public libraries, the school library sector, libraries in the health sector, libraries in the voluntary sector, and industrial and commercial libraries. Details are given on p.28.

This guide attempts to explain how the Copyright, Designs and Patents Act 1988, hereafter referred to as 'the Act', affects librarians and information workers and offers guidance on interpreting the main provisions of the law. Where appropriate, references are made to numbered sections of the Act. The Act took effect from August 1989 and applies throughout the UK. Many of the definitions are scattered throughout the Act. Some of the terms are undefined leaving them open to be dealt with by case law, agreement with copyright-owner representatives, or by common sense. The Act and relevant Statutory Instruments should be consulted for more detail when required. It should be borne in mind that the law, agreements with rights owners and licensing schemes are all subject to change. Any changes will be reported in the *Library Association record*.

Library and information service professionals, as guardians of intellectual property, recognize and are committed to support their users' need to gain access to copyright works and the information and ideas they contain. Although LIS professionals cannot act as copyright police, it is important that, whilst encouraging access, every effort should be made to protect and encourage respect for intellectual property. LIS professionals could be seen to be encouraging copyright infringement if there appeared to be no barrier to prevent infringing copies being made in the library or information unit. For instance, if there is a self-service photocopier in the library it is extremely important that the advice given on p.24 – **Self-service photocopiers and liability** – is observed.

Copyright: the main provisions of the Act

What is copyright?

Copyright gives legal protection to the creators of certain kinds of material so that they can control the way their work may be exploited. Copyright protection is automatic and there is no registration or other formality. Copyright law is also concerned to find a balance between the legitimate interests of creators who wish to be rewarded for the reproduction of their works, and the needs of users to have access to their works.

Materials subject to copyright

Copyright subsists in the following works:

(a) 'original literary, dramatic, musical or artistic works'
Computer programs are protected as literary works; tables and compilations (databases) are also included here; some databases are protected as 'cable programme services'.

(b) 'sound recordings, films, broadcasts or cable programmes'
Films include any kind of video recording.

(c) 'typographical arrangements of published editions'.

Length of the copyright period

From 1 January 1996, the duration of the copyright period has been extended. One of the conditions of the extended term is that authors have to be European Economic Area (EEA) nationals. Not all the conditions can be reproduced in this short guide. Please refer to SI 1995:3297 for exact conditions. See also EU Directive on the **Extension of the term of protection** on p.17.

Literary, dramatic, musical or artistic works

Copyright expires 70 years after the end of the year of a known author's death; *or* for works of unknown authorship, expiry is 70 years from the end of the calendar year in which the work was made; *or* 70 years from when the work was first made available to the public. *Made available to the public* of a literary, dramatic or musical work includes publication and the performance or inclusion of such works in a broadcast or cable programme service. For an artistic work, it includes being exhibited in public, included in a film being shown to the public or included in a broadcast or cable programme service.

Photographs deserve special attention as they may not conform to the above. Photographs taken by whatever process on or after 1 August 1989 are protected for 70 years after the death of the photographer unless they are subject to Crown, Parliamentary or international organizations copyright. If Crown copyright applies (and this is the same for all literary, dramatic, musical or artistic works),

protection is for a maximum of 125 calendar years. If published commercially within 75 calendar years of taking, Crown copyright exists for only 50 calendar years from the end of the year in which the photograph was created. Photographs subject to Parliamentary copyright are protected for 50 calendar years from taking. Photographs whose copyright belongs to any of the international organizations recognized for this purpose by UK law (i.e. UNESCO, etc.) are protected for 50 calendar years from the end of the year in which the photograph was taken.

Films

Copyright expires 70 years after the death of the last to die of the following: the principal director, the author of the screenplay, the author of the dialogue or the composer of the music created for and used in the film.

Sound recordings, broadcasts, cable programmes and computer generated works

Copyright expires 50 years after the end of the year in which they were made, released or first broadcast or included in a cable programme service. A sound recording is *released* when it is first published, played in public, broadcast or included in a cable programme service. The latter term applies to services accessible via a public telecommunications system, and the term may cover certain kinds of online database.

Typographical arrangements of published works

Copyright expires 25 years after the end of the year in which the edition was first published.

Who owns the copyright?

For literary, dramatic, musical or artistic works, the creator(s) of the work owns the copyright. This could be the author, artist, photographer, playwright, composer et al. In the case of computer-generated work, the author is the person who undertakes the arrangements necessary for the creation of the work.

Copyright is owned by the employer if the work is made in the course of employment, unless the contract specifies otherwise.

In the case of a sound recording or film, copyright is owned by the person who undertakes the arrangements necessary for the making of the recording (usually the producer) or film (usually the director, but see above for duration of copyright for **Films**); for broadcasts, it is the person who makes the broadcast; and in the case of a cable programme, the person who provides the service in which the programme is included.

For typographical arrangements of published works, it is the publisher.

It is important to note that those listed above are the initial owners of the copyright. These rights may be assigned or sold to other persons or organizations.

Copyright restrictions

The owners of copyright have exclusive rights to their works. Anyone who does any of the following without permission or licence is infringing copyright apart from the specific exceptions allowed under the Act. Unless otherwise permitted or licensed, only rights owners are allowed:

- **to copy the work [S.17]**
  Copying means reproducing a work in any material form and includes storing the work in any medium by electronic means. With regard to artistic works, it is also a restricted act to make a copy in three dimensions of a two-dimensional work and make a copy in two dimensions of a three-dimensional work. It is also an infringement to make a copy which is transient or incidental to some other use of the work.
- **to issue copies of the work to the public [S.18]**
  This means the right to publish or not. It also includes rental and lending of copies to the public.
- **to perform, show or play the work in public [S.19]**
  A performance includes delivery of a lecture, speech or sermon as well as a visual or acoustic presentation using a sound recording, film, broadcast or cable programme (this could be over an electronic network). The playing or showing of the work in public is also not allowed without permission.
- **to broadcast the work or include it in a cable programme service [S.20]**
- **to make an adaptation of the work or do any of the above in relation to the adaptation [SS.16–21]**
  This means adapting a literary, dramatic or musical work into a different format e.g. from a novel into a play, or making a translation from one language to another.

What is copyright infringement?

Infringement can occur only if more than a 'substantial part' is involved. However, although undefined in the Act, this has been established by case law as turning upon significance of content as well as extent. Therefore almost anything could be judged 'substantial' in particular circumstances. For example, copying a two page summary and recommendations of a 100 page report may be judged substantial in certain cases. Similarly, copying a segment of a photograph or a detail from some other form of artistic work may also be regarded as a 'substantial part'.

Secondary infringement [SS.22–26]

Unless specific permission is granted, it is not permitted to import infringing copies into the UK (other than for private or domestic use). The Act also forbids possession in the course of business, selling, hiring (or offering to do so), or otherwise distributing infringing copies to such an extent that it damages the copyright owners' entitlement.

A copy made for a purpose allowed under the Act can automatically become an infringing copy if used in other circumstances. For example, a copy quite legitimately made for an examination question could become an infringing copy if used for another purpose [S.27].

It is an infringement to provide the means specifically designed for making infringing copies, if it is known (or there is a reason to believe) that it will be used to make infringing copies. An obvious example would be a set of printing plates to print banknotes.

Without the licence of the copyright owner, it is an infringement to transmit a work by means of a telecommunications system (otherwise than by broadcasting or inclusion in a cable programme service) knowing or having reason to believe that infringing copies of the work will be made by the recipients of the transmission.

Persons may be liable for infringement if they permit premises to be used, or provide equipment, for an infringing performance of a copyright literary, dramatic or musical work, unless there are grounds for believing that the performance will not infringe. This refers to the playing of sound recordings, showing of films (videos) or receiving visual images or sounds conveyed by electronic means.

Moral rights

Moral rights belong to authors and are independent of the economic rights of copyright. It is important to be aware of them as they become increasingly relevant in the digital environment. The four moral rights are:

1 **The right of paternity**
  This is the right of the author to be identified as such. This right has to be asserted and a statement to this effect is to be found on the title page verso of many publications and on the backs of photographs or the mounts of transparencies or slides. There are exceptions to this right e.g. the right does not apply to computer programs, design of typefaces and computer-generated works. Nor does it apply to works generated in the course of employment [S.77–79].
2 **The right of integrity**
  This is the right of the author to prevent or object to derogatory treatment of his/her work [S.80]. *Treatment* is defined to mean an addition, deletion from or alteration to or adaptation of the work. (Adaptation in this sense does not apply to a translation of a literary, dramatic or musical work.) The treatment of a work would be seen as *derogatory* if it is distorted or mutilated or is otherwise seen as being prejudicial to the honour or reputation of the author.
3 **The right of false attribution**
  This is the right of a person not to have a literary, dramatic, musical or artistic work falsely attributed to him/her as an author [S.84].
4 **The right of disclosure**
  This is the right of the author to withhold certain

photographs or films from publication. Under the UK Act this would apply to a person who commissions the work but decides not to have it issued to the public; exhibited or shown in public; or included in a broadcast or cable programme [S.85].

Penalties

Although the Act refers to 'criminal liability', this is likely to apply to deliberate infringement for business purposes. The most likely penalties for infringing copyright are: (a) an injunction to prevent further infringement; (b) an instruction to 'deliver up' infringing copies to the rights owners; and (c) the award of damages. Rights owners are thus able to institute proceedings against alleged infringement in the Magistrates' Courts rather than the High Court. It is recommended that **SS.107–115** are studied in order to understand the possible consequences of infringement. Similar penalties and procedures apply under Scottish law. See also the section on **Case law** on p.26.

Exceptions to exclusive rights

Under the terms of the Berne Convention, the main international copyright convention, signatory nations may grant certain exceptions to the exclusive rights of authors, within limitations. Each signatory nation is allowed to authorize the reproduction of copyright works in 'certain special cases' provided that such reproduction does not conflict with the normal exploitation of the work, and does not unreasonably prejudice the legitimate interests of the author. In the UK, the main exceptions are covered by a general right to copy called fair dealing, copying for educational purposes and copying by librarians and archivists.

NB: a copy made under these exceptions must not be subsequently 'dealt with' which means it must not be sold or used for purposes other than those specified, otherwise it becomes an infringing copy.

Fair dealing

Fair dealing is an undefined term which does not in itself give specific permission to copy. It is really a defence that could be used by a person accused of infringement if the case were taken to court. Fair dealing only applies to specific purposes: research or private study (which implies no publication); criticism or review (whether for publication or not); or news reporting (not photographs). *Dealing* does not necessarily mean a transaction, nor need it apply only to copying. It is rather a form of general behaviour. *Fair* could only be decided in court in respect of specific circumstances and works. It is taken to mean, however, that *fair* dealing would not unfairly deprive owners of copyright a reasonable financial return on their property.

Fair dealing: research or private study [S.29]

Anyone may copy from literary, dramatic, musical or artistic works, including typographical arrangements, as long as it is (a) fair and (b) for research or private study. *Private study* is undefined but it obviously excludes group or class study; and *research* covers any kind including that undertaken for commercial or industrial purposes. The amount that may be copied is not specified nor is the number of copies. However, if a person copies on another's behalf, only one copy may be made. Any library may also copy on behalf of an individual under this provision (as well as under the library regulations) but a library must not use fair dealing in order to exceed the extents copiable from literary, dramatic or musical works [S.29(3)]. Fair dealing includes artistic works, whereas the library regulations do not. All librarians, whether copying under fair dealing or the library regulations should follow the advice under **Guidance on copying limits** on p.11. Librarians are not allowed to make multiple copies under the provisions of the library regulations.

Fair dealing: criticism or review [S.30(1)]

Anyone may copy from any type of work for the purposes of criticism or review provided sufficient acknowledgment is given. It is implied that making multiple copies for publication (i.e. a quotation) for this purpose is permitted. For quotations, the accepted limits are: one extract of no more than 400 words; several extracts none more than 300 words and totalling no more than 800 words; or up to 40 lines from a poem. It cannot be assumed that it is acceptable to copy the typographical layout under this provision. Nor can it be assumed that copying an artistic work by one author whilst criticizing or reviewing the work of another is acceptable, unless there is an obvious, necessary and direct link between them. In other words, genuine comparison of artistic works is acceptable, merely generically illustrative or visually exciting use of photography or film, depicting say, one version of a play or operatic production whilst commenting on a new presentation of the same is not.

Fair dealing: news reporting [S.30(2)]

Anyone may copy from a work (but not photographs) for the purposes of reporting current events, other than reporting done by means of a sound recording, film, broadcast or cable programme, provided sufficient acknowledgment of the source is given. It is implied that making multiple copies for publication (i.e. a quotation) for this purpose is permitted. It cannot be assumed that it is acceptable to copy the typographical layout under this provision.

Incidental inclusion [S.31]

If a copyright work is included incidentally in an artistic work, sound recording, film, broadcast or cable programme, copyright is not infringed. An example of this might be the making of a video in which a work of art was on display.

Copying by librarians and archivists

On 1 August 1989, regulations came into force for librarians and archivists, (and those acting on their behalf) under sections 37–43. These regulations (SI 1989:1212), known as the 'library regulations' or 'library privileges', apply to library staff who carry out photocopying on behalf of their users and for other libraries. **For users copying on self-service photocopiers, the fair dealing notes apply** (see above). All librarians and information staff should study a copy of these regulations.

It is important to note that the regulations apply to the copying of literary, dramatic or musical works but not artistic, although an illustration may be copied if it accompanies a work. Librarians who provide a staffed photocopying service are obliged under the Act to provide photocopy declaration forms for users to sign. A copy of the prescribed declaration form is given in Appendix B (this form may be copied freely). Librarians must be satisfied that these declaration forms are valid, insofar as this is possible, which throws responsibility on library staff. However, staff cannot be expected to check records retrospectively. The LA therefore considers that recognition of duplicate requests must be left to the memory of the staff concerned. Nonetheless, the Act implies that librarians will act responsibly and it is important to make a positive effort to reflect this trust.

FE and HE library and information units, provided that they are non-profit based services, are *prescribed* for the purposes of: providing a copying service to the public under SS.38, 39 and 43; and for copying for archival or preservation purposes covered by SS.41 and 42, whether within their own stock, made for another non-profit based service, or received from any other library. Please see Appendix A for a full list of prescribed libraries.

Note also the following:

- Any UK library can act as an intermediary, and make and supply copies in response to research or private study requests from individuals via other libraries.
- Profit-based libraries or archives are prescribed to copy for other libraries under **SS.41, 42 and 43** but may not receive copies for their own stock.
- Non-profit based libraries outside the UK are prescribed for receiving copies made for them by a UK library under **SS.41 and 42**.
- Any UK library, including a profit-based service, can copy on behalf of individuals under fair dealing **[S.29]**.

Copying service (local or interlibrary document supply) [SS.38–40]

Librarians may provide a copying service, in response to local or interlibrary requests from individuals, subject to the following conditions. NB: copying is for the purposes of research or private study only and that *research* embraces all kinds of research, including commercial research, *private study* excludes class or group study.

The requirements are:

(a) that the requester signs a form declaring that:

- a copy of the same material has not previously been supplied by any librarian;
- the material is for the purposes of research or private study only;
- the requester is not aware that any other person has requested or is about to request a copy of substantially the same material for substantially the same purpose;

(b) that the librarian does not get requests for substantially the same material at substantially the same time (these terms are not defined);

(c) that no more than one copy of an article per periodical issue or no more than a reasonable proportion from a published work is requested; (*reasonable proportion* is undefined but it is suggested that the guidelines on p.11 are followed);

(d) that the librarian makes a charge for the copy to recover the costs of production, together with a contribution towards the general expenses of the library. (See **Charging for copying** on p.20.)

Interlibrary copying for stock [S.41]

Librarians are also allowed to make and supply to a non-profit-based library, a copy of any article in a periodical or, as the case may be, of the whole or part of a published edition of a literary, dramatic or musical work for stock required by that other library, subject to the following conditions:

(a) that the requesting library is not furnished with more than one copy of the same article or of the whole or part of the published edition;

(b) that where the request is for more than one article from a periodical, or the whole or part of a published edition, the requesting library satisfies the librarian (in a *written* statement) that they do not know and are unable to find out the name and address of the person or persons who could authorize the copying (e.g. an out-of-print item whose publisher is no longer in business);

(c) that the librarian makes a charge for the copy to recover the costs of production, together with a contribution towards the general expenses of the library. (See **Charging for copying** on p.20.)

Copying for replacement [S.42]

Librarians of non-profit based libraries may also make copies of items in order to replace them in the permanent collection of their library or archive or in the permanent collection of another non-profit based library or archive, subject to the following conditions:

(a) that the item is held in the permanent collection for reference only, or is held in the permanent collection and is available for loan only to other libraries for reference purposes;

(b) that it is not reasonably practical for the item to be purchased (e.g. an out-of-print item);

(c) that if the copy is for another library, then the other library must declare in a *written* statement:

- that the copy has been lost, destroyed or damaged;
- that it is not reasonably practical to purchase a replacement;
- that the copy will be for reference purposes only;

(d) that the librarian makes a charge for the copy to recover the costs of production, together with a contribution towards the general expenses of the library. (See **Charging for copying** on p.20.)

Copying unpublished works [S.43]

Librarians of non-profit based libraries are also allowed to copy the whole or part of certain unpublished literary, dramatic or musical works from documents held in the library or archive, subject to the following conditions:

(a) that the requester signs a form declaring that:

- a copy of the same material has not previously been supplied by any librarian;
- the material is for the purposes of research or private study only;
- that the requester is reasonably sure that the document has not been published prior to being deposited in the library or archive, and that the copyright owner has not prohibited the copying of the work;

(b) that only one copy is supplied to the requester;

(c) that the librarian makes a charge for the copy to recover the costs of production, together with a contribution towards the general expenses of the library. (See **Charging for copying** on p.20.)

Special rules for education [S.32–35]

Copying for instruction [S.32]

The Act says that it is permitted to copy from a literary, dramatic, musical or artistic work in the course of instruction or preparation for instruction provided it is done by the person giving or receiving instruction, and not copied by means of a reprographic process. A *reprographic process* is defined as a process for making facsimile copies or which involves the use of an appliance for making multiple copies. This indicates that copying from copyright material for class purposes is only allowed if it is done in longhand and not on a photocopier.

If the educational establishment is licensed (see **Copyright Licensing Agency licensing schemes** on p.14) then photocopying for class use is allowed, subject to the restrictions of the licence. If no licence is available, teachers may copy 1% of any work in any quarterly period, i.e. 1 January–31 March, 1 April–30 June, etc. **[S.36]**.

Copying for examinations [S.32(3)]

The Act says that it is not an infringement to copy for the purposes of examination by way of setting the questions, communicating the questions to the candidates, or answering the questions apart from the reprographic copying of a musical work for use by an examination candidate in performing the work. *Purposes of examination* is not defined but it is unlikely that this exemption applies to work continuously assessed as part of the examination process. Copies made for this purpose must not be subsequently 'dealt with', i.e. the external publication or distribution of collections of past examination papers or extracts from them containing parts of copyright material would be an infringement.

Performing a literary, dramatic or musical work [S.34]

Permission is also given to educational establishments to play or show a sound recording, film or video, broadcast or cable programme to audiences of lecturers and students in the activities of the establishment or for the purposes of instruction (see **Videos** on p.25). Permission has to be sought from rights owners if a performance is to be public (see also **Playing music in educational establishments** on p.24). NB: Artistic works do not need permission because their display or exhibition does not infringe copyright.

Off-air recording [S.35]

Off-air recording from broadcasts or cable programmes (radio and television) may be made by or on behalf of an educational establishment without infringing copyright unless there is a licensing scheme available. At present there are two licensing schemes. Please see p.15 for details. Also, satellite and cable channels, provided they are legitimately received, may be recorded for educational purposes as there is no licensing scheme available.

Copying audiovisual material for teaching film and sound recording production [S.32(2)]

Sound recordings, films, broadcasts and cable programmes may be copied by making a film or sound track in the course of or in preparation for instruction in the making of films or film sound tracks, provided the copying is done by the person giving or receiving instruction.

Other exceptions and permissions

Abstracts [S.60]
Abstracts accompanying scientific or technical articles in periodicals may be copied and issued to the public, unless there is a licensing scheme available. No licensing scheme exists at present.

Advertising art works for sale [S.63]
Copies may be made and issued to the public of artistic works in order to advertise them for sale. This would include the compilation of such works in a catalogue.

Anonymous works [S.57]
Copying is allowed from a work which, after reasonable enquiry, is believed to be anonymous, and where it is reasonable to assume the copyright has expired or that the author died over 70 years ago.

Free public showing or playing of a broadcast or cable programme [S.72]
As long as the public is not charged for admission to wherever the showing is to take place, this is allowed.

Off-air recording [S.70]
The private and domestic copying of a broadcast or cable programme (i.e. making a video of a TV programme, or a tape of a radio programme, for use at a more convenient time) is allowed. This is familiarly called time-shifting. This provision does not allow libraries to record programmes. See **Off-air recording licensing schemes** on p.15.

Parliamentary and judicial proceedings [S.45]
Copyright is not infringed by copying for the purposes of Parliamentary or judicial proceedings.

Photograph of a television broadcast or cable programme [S.71]
A photograph or slide may be made of the whole or part of an image forming part of a television broadcast or cable programme for private and domestic use.

Playing of sound recordings in clubs [S.67]
Clubs or societies which are not conducted for profit, and whose main objects are charitable or otherwise concerned with the advancement of religion, education or social welfare, are allowed to play sound recordings, provided any charge for admission is applied solely for the purposes of the organization.

Provision of subtitled copies of broadcast and cable programmes [S.74]
The National Subtitling Library for Deaf People has been designated by the Secretary of State for Trade and Industry to make copies of broadcasts or cable programmes in order to adapt them for the needs of the deaf and hard of hearing. The Act also allows modification for designating a body to cover other disabilities such as physical or learning disability, but there has been no relevant designation as yet.

Public inspection [S.47]
Material open to public inspection for statutory purposes (e.g. planning documents lodged with a local authority, or electoral registers) may be copied, subject to certain conditions.

Reading in public [S.59]
The reading or recitation in public by one person of a reasonable extract from a published literary or dramatic work does not infringe copyright if it is acknowledged. It would be wise to obtain permission from the publishers in the case of formally organized events as opposed to informal readings.

Royal Commission or statutory enquiry [S.46]
Copyright is not infringed by anything done for the purposes of the proceedings of a Royal Commission or statutory enquiry.

Guidance on copying limits

The Library Association recommends that copying under fair dealing for research or private study observes the same limits set down by the library regulations.

Number of copies
Anyone copying on behalf of someone else for research or private study is restricted to making one copy. Persons copying for themselves do not appear to be so restricted, but may have to defend 'fairness' to the copyright owner. An example of a situation in which two copies *might* be regarded as *fair* might be a person studying a subject which required a visit to a geological site. One copy of a portion of a map or chart might be required to carry out the visit and another might be required to record the results of the visit. It may also apply to photographs used for site inspection or planning of some kind.

Published literary works

Periodicals
Librarians of non-profit based libraries are restricted to copying only one article from any periodical issue for their

users [S.38(1)]. Accordingly, The Library Association recommends that users making their own copies (under fair dealing for research or private study) should not exceed the same limit.

An article is defined as 'any item'. When several small items appear together (e.g. news items without separate authors), they may be treated as one item unless they form an unreasonable proportion of the periodical issue. For example, it would be unreasonable to expect a user to ensure that a copy was not made of several unwanted items printed on an A4 page alongside the item one required. A contents page counts, however, as one item (see **Contents pages** on p.21).

Books

The library regulations state that a reasonable proportion may be copied. No statutory guidance is given for copying under fair dealing for research or private study. It is generally agreed that no more than one complete chapter or a maximum otherwise of 5% of the work is reasonable.

Short books, reports or pamphlets without chapters

The Library Association recommends that up to 10% of a work is reasonable for short works provided that the extract does not amount to more than 20 pages.

Poems, short stories and other short literary works

These are whole works in themselves and therefore should not be copied without permission but when in collections or anthologies, a short story or poem of not more than 10 pages may be copied. A poem or short story, whose author is out of copyright, contained in a collection or anthology published over 25 years ago may be copied. Poems embedded in a chapter of a book may be treated as part of the chapter.

British Standards

The BSI has agreed that up to 10% of a Standard may be copied. This amount is the same for copying from a printed Standard, microform or CD-ROM.

Crown and Parliamentary publications including HMSO material

HMSO has published a third in the series of 'Dear Librarian' letters dated April 1995 which clarifies what may be copied from Crown and Parliamentary copyright publications without seeking permission. A copy of this letter is available from HMSO. (See list of useful addresses in Appendix C). The objective of the Copyright Unit at HMSO is to 'facilitate the widest possible dissemination of official material, while ensuring that all reproduction is proper and appropriate in the general public interest.' HMSO believes that it is in the public interest that this

material is widely available so considerable freedom to photocopy is allowed, as long as copying is not for personal gain or commercial profit (if it is, then HMSO's 'Dear Publisher' letter applies), from the following categories of material:

- Lords and Commons Official Reports (Hansard), Bills of Parliament, and House Business Papers, including Journals of both Houses, Lords Minutes, the Vote Bundle, Commons Order-Books, the Commons Public Bill Lists and Statutory Instruments Lists, the Weekly Information Bulletin and the Sessional Information Digest, all of which are Parliamentary copyright;
- other Parliamentary papers published by HMSO, including Command Papers and Reports of Select Committees of both Houses;
- Acts of Parliament, Statutory Instruments and Statutory Rules and Orders, which are Crown copyright;
- press releases from departments, agencies or other Crown bodies. (While these are obviously for unrestricted use at time of issue, they may be freely reproduced thereafter.)

It is permitted without formal permission or charge:

(a) to copy any single title or document in its entirety provided that:

- no more than one photocopy is made for any one individual;
- no more than one photocopy is used within any one organization;
- copies are not distributed to other individuals or organizations;

(b) to make multiple photocopies of:

- a number of extracts from a single work amounting in total to no more than 30% of the entire work, or
- one complete single chapter or equivalent, even if more than 30% of the complete work,
- in either case, copies may be provided to others.

For other Crown and Parliamentary copyright material published by HMSO, copying should be restricted to the recommended limits for research or private study in respect of books, pamphlets and reports.

HMSO makes it clear in the letter that photocopying is NOT allowed in connection with advertising or endorsement, nor in circumstances which may be 'potentially libellous or slanderous of individuals, companies or organizations'. This is particularly relevant to Parliamentary material 'whose use must not give rise to unfair or misleading selection or undignified association'. It is also pointed out that Hansard enjoys special protection from proceedings for defamation. Anyone publishing non-official copies of proceedings in Parliament would not enjoy this protection.

Official Journal of the EU

A generous attitude is adopted towards copying from the Official Journal as, similar to copying from Crown and Parliamentary material, it is in the EU interest to disseminate the information contained therein. The LA has obtained oral assurance that copying is allowed from this publication for research and educational purposes. No definite limits were given.

Yellow Pages

BT, which owns the rights in the Yellow Pages directories, has confirmed that under fair dealing for research or private study purposes, a maximum of one page or one classified section (whichever is the smaller) may be copied from Yellow Pages. Library users may therefore copy this amount for themselves. If a librarian does the copying for the user, then more may be copied. The LA recommends that copying should not be more than 5% and users should sign a copyright declaration form. Users needing to copy more than 5% should be advised to contact BT for permission. BT are also able to supply business mailing lists. (See Appendix C for contact details.)

Artistic works

Artistic works may not be copied under the library regulations. Copying under fair dealing is allowed although, like all fair dealing, may be subject to a challenge of 'fairness'. It is advised that copying whole works should be done only if permission or licence has been granted.

Illustrations

These may be copied only if they illustrate or form part of an article from a periodical or are included in extracts from other material. Discretion should be used when copying them on their own since they may be complete works in themselves.

Ordnance Survey maps

Even though librarians are not given statutory permission to copy artistic works under the library regulations, Ordnance Survey has signed an agreement with The Library Association, Joint Consultative Committee and the British Committee for Map Information and Cataloguing Systems (BRICMICS) to allow librarians to copy OS maps for their users subject to certain conditions. Requests must be accompanied by a copyright declaration form and meet the other conditions specified in the library regulations. The maximum amount which may be copied is four copies of a single extract from an Ordnance Survey or OS-based map not exceeding 625 sq cms (A4 size). These must be straight scale copies i.e. they may not be enlarged. The same amount may be copied by a person

copying for themselves under fair dealing for the purposes of research or private study.

Digital mapping: Libraries may provide printed extracts from OS digital mapping to users on the same basis as they provide photocopies from a hard copy.

See also **Ordnance Survey education licences, p.16.**

Goad plans

Chas E. Goad supply their retail plans to public libraries with a licence to copy. Permission is given to copy for students only provided evidence is given, such as a student card or other acceptable form of identification, e.g. a college letterhead confirming their attendance at that establishment. Goad has stipulated that copies may not be made for any other purpose. It is advised that colleges should make this arrangement and the conditions known to their students. The amount allowed to be copied is the same as from an OS map – up to four copies of a single extract not exceeding A4 (625 sq cms). Students will be required to sign a form declaring that the copy is for research or private study purposes only.

Photographs

Photographs, unlike literary or musical works, do not easily conform to the extract, proportional copying or quotation rules since, in many instances and especially in the case of vertical aerial photographs, even a segment from an original photograph can produce an image which is considered a complete work in itself. This indivisibility of visual materials has led to the situation where it is generally acceptable to rights holders for complete photographs to be copied in the following circumstances: under fair dealing for research or private study; when the copy is of a lesser resolution quality than the original; when the image is defaced or clearly marked in some way; or the characteristics of the copied image clearly indicate that it is a derivative and not a first generation item from the creator's original work. Whatever the resolution quality of the copy, individuals may make copies of photographs for their own private and domestic use. Individuals may make copies of photographs provided the rights owner has not prohibited copying of the work.

Slides or transparencies

There is no statutory provision for copying illustrations or diagrams as whole works. However, it is The LA's view that one copy, but not photographic works, may be made to accompany a lecture provided that it cannot be purchased from a commercial source. However, such copies may not be deposited in the library. Making transparencies from illustrations, photographs or plates in books or other published works for library collections is almost certainly likely to infringe the Act. Unless licensed to do so (see **DACS slide licensing scheme** on p.15), it is advisable to include in slide collections only: transparencies purchased from a commercial source, those made with the permission of the rights owner and those made from sources which are out of copyright.

Music

The fair dealing exception for copying for research or private study applies to printed music. Librarians may also make and supply a copy of a part of a musical work under the library regulations.

The Code of Fair Practice agreed between composers and publishers of printed music states that 'bona fide students or teachers, whether they are in an educational establishment or not may, without application to the copyright owner, make copies of short excerpts of musical works provided that they are for study only (not for performance). Copying whole movements or whole works is expressly forbidden under this permission'. This booklet also outlines other permissions to copy for specific circumstances. See the *Code of fair practice for printed music* (revised edition) Music Publishers' Association (address in Appendix C).

Licensing

The UK Act encourages the use of the law of contract for collective licensing. Licensing 'schemes', must cover works of more than one author. The ideal 'blanket licensing' to cover all materials of interest to a user group has not been achieved. Contracts such as licences are a matter for agreement between parties, normally outside legislation. Contract law can override copyright law. However, an important feature of the Act is the establishment of a Copyright Tribunal to arbitrate on the terms and conditions of licensing schemes. As yet, it has not been convened to arbitrate in any licensing scheme affecting the library and information or teaching professions.

Copyright Licensing Agency licensing schemes

The main licensing body for reprographic copying from most UK books and periodicals, and those of an increasing number of other countries with which it has reciprocal agreements, is the Copyright Licensing Agency (CLA) (address in Appendix C). The CLA acts mainly as agent for the Authors' Licensing and Collecting Society and the Publishers' Licensing Society. Most LEA schools and colleges of further education, all universities and institutes of higher education, many schools and colleges in the independent sector, some Government departments, some industry sectors and commercial companies are licensed by the Copyright Licensing Agency to make multiple copies within clearly defined limits from most books, journals and periodicals.

It is essential for library managers to see this licence and also to obtain copies of the CLA User Guidelines and Notice to Teaching and Administrative Staff, circulated by the CLA to institutions after being agreed with the representatives on the Committee of Vice-Chancellors and Principals, the Association for Colleges and the College Employers Forum. The licence should be held in the administration department of the institution concerned. A summary of the licensing conditions for FE and HE is outlined below.

The CLA has a list of excluded categories and works which should be checked before copying. This does not always mean that these works may not be copied. Some works may be covered by another licence. An excluded work or category may also mean that the copyright owner will allow copying to a greater extent than under fair dealing or the library regulations.

NB: when no licence is available, teachers may copy for instruction purposes 1% of material in any quarterly period (see **Copying for instruction** on p.10).

Further education licence

This current licence term was due to expire on 31 July 1995 but has been extended until July 1996 pending negotiation for a further term. The terms of the licence described here may therefore be subject to change.

The basic licence allows the making and receiving of multiple copies by authorized persons (all staff and students) of any one item of copyright material for any one course of study or for use in formal instruction or study within that course. Copying must only be undertaken on the licensed premises. The amount copied must not exceed 5% of extracts or one chapter from a published copyright work or a single article from one serial publication or set of conference proceedings.

The Agreement allows the copying and creation of material for use in study or course packs (loose-leaf or bound) within strict limits. For copying and assembling extracts of copyright material in sets of five or more, each containing more than four items, during any one course of study, permission must be sought from CLARCS – the CLA Rapid Clearance System. These packs may only be sold to staff or students at a price to recoup the cost of production and not intended to make a profit. The front cover should contain a prominent notice to point out that the packs may not be re-sold or copied further.

A sample of institutions is selected to take part in a survey which entails keeping records of copies made under the licence. The purpose of the survey is to monitor the operation of the licence and to calculate fees due to copyright owners/licensees. (This should exclude copies made under the fair dealing provisions or under the library regulations.)

Higher education licence

This current licence term, due to expire on 31 July 1995, has been extended until July 1996 on existing terms pending negotiation. The terms described here may be subject to change.

The licence permits the reproduction within specified limits of materials published in most books, periodicals and journals published in the UK, USA, France, Spain, Germany, Australia, Canada, Norway, Sweden, South Africa and New Zealand, for 'any occasion or purpose' including multiple copying for purposes of a lecture, seminar, tutorial or similar class. The number of copies made may not exceed the number of students in a class, together with a copy for the person teaching, and must be made on the licensed premises.

This is not a licence for unlimited copying; it is limited in terms of quantities and extents. It permits all staff and students to copy 'for any one course of study in one academic year' extracts of up to 5% or one complete chapter of books or up to the whole of an article in journals and periodicals. Some categories of works and certain titles are excluded from the licence.

A Supplemental Agreement excludes from the basic licence the making of collections of photocopies of extracts from copyright materials, 'compiled in advance' to create course readers, or study packs, whether looseleaf or bound. Unless fewer than five compilations, each consisting of fewer than four separate extracts, are being assembled, permission must be sought and payment made via CLARCS – the CLA Rapid Clearance System. Study packs created with CLARCS clearance may be sold to students, but at prices designed only to recoup production costs. Study packs may not be re-sold nor may the contents be photocopied further.

Institutions may be selected to participate in photocopying surveys (replacing the previous sample recording scheme), to monitor operation of the licence and to provide data for calculation of fees payable by Collecting Societies. Care should be taken to distinguish between licensed copying and copies made under the fair dealing and library copying provisions of the Act.

BL/CLA agreement
The British Library Document Supply Centre (BLDSC) has a licensing agreement with the CLA to provide a copyright cleared service. This licence allows the supply of copyright material to libraries over and above the limitations of the library regulations and so removes the conditions of supply, permits longer extracts and more copies, and more than one extract from the same issue of a journal. The BL states that the copies supplied may not be copied further by the individual recipient.

DACS slide licensing scheme
The problem of not being legally authorized to make slides of copies of artistic works in published editions and build up a collection of such slides for use in education has been addressed by the Design and Artists' Copyright Society (DACS). DACS is the collecting society representing the interests of visual artists including commercial artists and photographers. With the guidance of a steering group of user representatives from ARLIS, Aslib AV Group, IIS and the LA, DACS has developed a blanket slide licensing scheme. The scheme is in two parts: an agreement to declare and pay for any existing collection; and an annual licence for making new slides.

Organizations with an existing collection, including any illegally produced slides, are required to declare the approximate number and pay a fee. This is a one-off payment to DACS which is calculated according to the size of the collection. In return for payment and compliance with the terms of the agreement, DACS indemnifies the institution against claims of copyright infringement by artists for their works held in collections.

The cost is based on the number of slides in an existing collection. The licence fee is charged annually. A fixed sum is payable for the first year and subsequent annual payments are calculated on the number of slides added to the collection during each year.

A licensed institution may make up to ten copies of artistic works (including artistic works in books) onto slides, acetates or transparencies for educational purposes. These may be stored in the library. Please apply to DACS for exact details of the scheme (address in Appendix C).

Off-air recording licensing schemes
There are two licensing schemes available for recording radio and television programmes for educational purposes: the licensing scheme from the Educational Recording Agency (ERA) to cover all terrestrial broadcasting with the exception of Open University programmes; and the Open University Educational Enterprises (OUEE) Licensing Scheme which covers only the Open University programmes (see Appendix C for addresses). Any off-air recording of terrestrial channels must be covered by one or other of these schemes. Satellite and cable channels are, at the time of writing, not covered by licences. Until they are, off-air recording for educational purposes is free.

ERA licence
Payment for this licence is according to the type of establishment and the number of its full-time (or equivalent) students. Once licensed, the educational establishment may designate individuals to make off-air recordings of radio or TV programmes both in the school and from home. Within the conditions of the licence, tapes may be copied further, used in class, catalogued and kept indefinitely in library collections, and loaned to students. Licensed institutions may also borrow and copy recordings belonging to other ERA licence holders. Refer to ERA for a copy of their useful little guide to the scheme (address in Appendix C).

OUEE licence

This scheme works differently from ERA. Payment depends on the total numbers of recordings which are kept for longer than 30 days. OUEE requires that each recording has to be registered. Each establishment then has 30 days in which to view and delete the recording to avoid having to pay. No loans for use off the premises are permitted.

Other licensing schemes

UK pilot site licence initiative

This agreement, negotiated by the HE funding bodies with four periodical publishers – Academic Press, Blackwell Publishers, Blackwell Science and the Institute of Physics Publishing – allows UK universities: up to 40% discount on their publications; free access to some or all of their electronic versions; and unrestricted photocopying of paper articles from the titles subscribed to for non-profit purposes. This also extends to study packs. This is a pilot project for three years beginning January 1996.

Ordnance Survey education licences

There are two schemes which apply to education:

1   LEA schools may copy for educational purposes under the Local Authority licence from OS mapping.
2   An educational licence for all educational establishments *except* LEA schools: university and higher education, independent sector, grant maintained sector, public and private sector. This licence is for copying OS mapping for educational purposes on educational premises only. Mapping held in public libraries may not be used for copying under this licence.

If copying is for a purpose other than educational, i.e. copying for inclusion in a prospectus, then an extra licence for business must be obtained from Ordnance Survey.

Universities with an OS licence have been offered the right to use certain OS digital mapping data, available from EDINA (Edinburgh University Data Library) by the Joint Information Systems Committee. Details are available from edina@ed.ac.uk.

British Standards Institution licence

This licence allows copying for class purposes (this is taken to include short loan copies). Special bulk discounts are available when whole documents are needed. Otherwise the licence permits copying of substantial portions of standard specifications, short of whole documents. Details from the British Standards Institution, see Appendix C for address.

Newspaper Licensing Agency

In January 1996, a new licensing scheme was launched for organizations to make multiple copies of articles from newspapers. The scheme is aimed mainly at commercial organizations and cuttings agencies but educational establishments, government departments, professional organizations and the public and voluntary sector are also able to be licensed if they make copies from the newspapers covered by the licence over and above the copying limits for research or private study. The newspapers covered by the scheme are: *Daily Mail, The Mail on Sunday, Evening Standard, Daily Express, Sunday Express, Daily Star, Financial Times, The Guardian, The Observer, Independent, Independent on Sunday, Daily Mirror, Sunday Mirror, The People, The Daily Telegraph, Sunday Telegraph*. Other newspapers may be added to this list from time to time. (News International Group and regional newspapers are not covered by the scheme.)

The fees charged are based on the type of licence and according to the type of organization. Schools, colleges and universities are charged an annual flat fee for the purposes of instruction, but a separate licence is required for copying for internal management purposes. The licence covers photocopying only. Like the CLA licence, it does not cover artistic works or electrocopying. If an organization wishes to copy and store for dissemination electronically, permission must be obtained from the individual newspaper publisher concerned.

Institutions wishing to make multiple copies from the above newspapers, should consider obtaining a licence. Full details are available from the NLA, (address in Appendix C).

Rental and lending

The Act of 1988 established a new and separate right for rental services [S.18] and rental included public lending. Lending will be separated from Rental with the implementation of the EU Directive on Rental and Lending. Colleges of FE and universities, along with other educational establishments are likely to be exempt from any lending restriction. See details under **Rental and Lending Directive** on p.17. However, at present, it is not at all clear whether educational establishments operating a lending service to non-students extra-murally and therefore to 'the public' will be subject to Lending Right.

EU Directives

Following the publication of a Green Paper in 1988, the Commission of the European Communities embarked on a programme to harmonize the various copyright laws of member states. The areas where harmonization was seen to be necessary were: computer programs, the term of protection, rental and lending and certain neighbouring rights, databases, private copying, satellite and cable broadcasting and moral rights. The following is a selection of those relevant to the library and information profession and the main implications.

Computer software

The law relating to computer programs was the subject of the first amendment to the 1988 Copyright Act. It was amended by SI 1992:3233 The Copyright (Computer Programs) Regulations 1992 to comply with EU Directive No. 91/250/EEC on Computer Software.

Without infringing copyright, a lawful user of a copy of a computer program is allowed:

- to make a back-up copy even if terms or conditions state otherwise
- to copy or adapt it, provided that the copying or adapting is necessary for lawful use and is not prohibited under contract
- to observe, study or test a program by any device or means
- to decompile the program to the extent necessary to achieve interoperabilty of an independently created program with other programs.

Extension of the term of protection

EU Directive 93/98/EEC on the Duration of Copyright directs member states to extend the term of protection for copyright literary, dramatic, musical and artistic works and films from 50 to 70 years after the year of the death of the author. This became law in the UK on 1 January 1996 with the Duration of Copyright and Rights in Performances Regulations 1995 [SI 1995:3297].

For existing works still in copyright on 31 December 1995, copyright protection has been extended for a further 20 years. Works for which copyright expired before 31 December 1995 in the UK, but which are still protected in another EU member state on 1 July 1995, have their copyright revived. Depending on the year of the author's death, this could mean up to another 20 years protection.

The owner of the extended copyright is the person who owned the copyright before 1 January 1996. The owner of the revived copyright is the person who owned the copyright immediately before it expired. This will exacerbate further the problems of tracing who owns the copyright since the rights could have been bequeathed to the author's estate or assigned to a publisher. The LA advises that when permission to copy is needed (e.g. when copying and supplying to another non-profit based library, see **Interlibrary copying for stock** on p.9) and after reasonable enquiry the owner of the copyright cannot be traced, then copying may take place. For *reasonable enquiry* see advice under **Photographs** on p.23.

Any copying or publishing of works which were once in the public domain and which have now had their copy-right revived will not be deemed to be infringing acts, provided notice of intention is given to the copyright owners. These acts will then be treated as having been licensed by the copyright owner subject to agreed payments of a reasonable royalty or remuneration. The Copyright Tribunal may be used if there is disagreement. It is assumed that if innocent copying took place by a user, which did not involve publication, a remuneration or royalty would not have to be paid.

Rental and Lending Directive

In 1992 the European Council adopted the Directive on Rental and Lending Right and on Certain Rights related to Copyright in the Field of Intellectual Property (92/100/EEC) This Directive has yet to be implemented into UK legislation. NB: educational establishments will probably be exempt from lending right, unless they lend to the public or provide a commercial service. The following is therefore given mainly for information.

Public lending has now been separated from commercial rental and there is a clear definition of lending:

any arrangement under which a copy of a work is made available for use for a limited period of time through an establishment which is accessible to the public for no direct or indirect economic or commercial advantage on terms that it will or may be returned but excludes any arrangement under which a copy of a work is made available:

(a) between establishments which are accessible to the public, or
(b) for on the spot reference, or
(c) for the purpose of performance in public, exhibition in public, broadcasting or inclusion in a cable programme service

and in respect of lending, payment of an amount which does not go beyond the operating costs of the establishment shall be regarded as being not for direct or indirect economic or commercial advantage.

The legislation extends exclusive rental and lending rights to all forms of copyright works and most artistic works. Exceptions can be made to this right as long as authors are remunerated for the use of their works. The UK has a Public Lending Right scheme which covers the lending of books, so traditional book lending in public libraries will not be affected, but public lending of sound recordings, films and computer programs and other works at present not subject to PLR, will be subject to this new law.

Legal protection of databases

The Internal Market Council of the EU adopted a common position on the protection of databases in late 1995. This was ratified in early 1996. The Government has two years in which to implement it into UK legislation. The

Directive covers the protection of databases whether in electronic or non-electronic form and introduces a new *sui generis* (unique) form of protection for 15 years for such databases which are considered to be non-original in the selection and arrangement of their contents. The term *database* is understood to include collections of works whether literary, artistic, musical or of other material such as texts, sounds, images, numbers, facts and data which are systematically or methodically arranged and can be individually accessed, so both print and electronic databases are covered by this definition. For example: this could be a multimedia product on CD-ROM, an online database, an encyclopaedia or even a telephone directory. However, it does not cover recordings of audiovisual, cinematographic, literary or musical works, such as films and sound recordings.

Under the present UK Act, databases are already protected as compilations and there is no criterion of originality necessary to obtain the full copyright protection of 70 years plus life, if there is a personal author(s) even for a telephone directory. It will be left to the discretion of each member state to decide whether to grant exceptions to allow copying for certain purposes e.g. fair dealing from both the copyright protected databases and from those protected under the *sui generis* right. The Directive gives scope for such exceptions. It is likely that there may be little change to the existing Act because of a provision which allows member states already protecting databases comparable to the *sui generis* right to retain the same exceptions. The LA will issue further guidance when the Directive is implemented into the UK.

Other EU Directives

The EU has indicated that a Draft Directive on Private Copying is planned to appear in early 1996. This recommends that all member states impose a levy on recording equipment (VCRs, tape recorders and maybe even photocopiers) as well as recording media (tapes, discs etc.). Most other member states already have such a levy. It is not at all clear how this approach could be reconciled with the Act's provision for licensing off-air recording, nor how the principle of subsidiarity might mitigate the consequences for UK institutions.

Electronic copyright

The contents of works which are 'published' in electronic format such as material on CD-ROMs, online databases, floppy disks etc. are protected in the same way as their printed equivalents. What is important is that, although with printed information one can use fair dealing and the library regulations as defences for copying, the LA believes it is doubtful, given the fears of rights owners listed below, whether this extends to electronic works. In most cases, anyway, service contracts override those defences.

The exclusive right of reproduction given to authors includes storing the work in electronic form. Much information is being published in electronic form and the need to take advantage of using the new technologies is growing in pressure. The LA believes that librarians and information professionals are responsible intermediaries and have a crucial role to play in both controlling and facilitating access to the growing number of local and remote electronic information resources. However, before they can fulfil this role there is a need for a recognition and understanding of their important position in the information chain and their need for statutory rights to use copyright material in all formats. The LA is campaigning for such rights and is working closely with other information professional bodies (see **LA/JCC Working Party on Copyright** on p.28), both nationally and internationally.

This is an international problem. The full use of the new technologies and telecommunications will not be realized until adequate protection and effective networks of control are built into national and international intellectual property legislations. It is probable therefore, that until the situation is resolved most copying and use of works in electronic form – electrocopying – will continue to be performed under the terms of a contract with rights owners. Some deals have been negotiated with rights owners and/or their representatives to allow the use of works in electronic form. These are usually very tightly controlled. The UK Pilot Site Licence Initiative (see p.16) is an example of such a scheme.

This section describes the problems and fears of rights owners about electrocopying and gives some guidance on staying legal.

Electrocopying

Electrocopying is a term which has not yet been defined satisfactorily in legislation by either the UK or the European Union. It is generally understood to cover the storage, display, dissemination, manipulation or reproduction of print-based copyright works into machine-readable form. This means:

- using an optical scanner or document image processor to convert copyright protected works into electronic format
- rekeying copyright works from paper format into a word-processor
- downloading from commercial databases into a paper format
- downloading copyright protected material from databases directly on to a computer to store for further use
- sending copyright electronic material around a local area network
- transmitting copyright protected works by e-mail
- sending copyright works by fax.

Rights owners are concerned to protect their works from misuse and abuse, as well as wishing to obtain a fair return on their intellectual output and/or economic investment. Rights owners are concerned about:

- Deliberate infringement of copyright for economic gain, i.e. piracy. This threatens their economic rights. Rights owners are reluctant to allow their works to be stored in digital form as it is difficult and sometimes impossible to control or detect the movement of works electronically. Rights owners fear, therefore, that they will lose control of their intellectual property. Once digitized and stored in a computer, works can be transferred unseen.
- Copying could become common practice owing to a lack of user understanding about copyright plus ready availability of facilities. Without local instruction and control, users are likely to assume that because these facilities exist there are no barriers to their use.
- Ease of transfer internationally. An author or a publisher will be reluctant to give *carte blanche* permission for a work to be electronically available without some guarantee that it will not be misused and abused, or sent around the network to countries where copyright protection is inadequate.
- Violation of an author's moral rights. Works can be manipulated easily while in electronic format which infringes the author's right of integrity and increases the risk of plagiarism.

Electrocopying guidelines

Computer programs
When purchasing computer software packages, libraries should consider the appropriate multi-user licence needed. Without such a licence, the software may be loaded on to one machine only.

Using optical scanners
There are basically two types of scanners: optical character recognition and page-image processor. The former allows individual words to be searched for and manipulated. In page scanning, the work cannot be altered easily but whole works, such as artistic works, photographs and journal articles can be scanned, stored and retrieved. The potential for storage and preservation of paper-based library materials is enormous. However, the scanning of copyright works is illegal and should not be done without permission from copyright owners. It is advised, therefore, that copying is limited to: those works with your own organization's copyright (including correspondence); those in the public domain (e.g. clip art); those for which copyright has lapsed; or those for which you have obtained permission or licence.

Rekeying from paper format into a word processor
This mainly applies to whole works or substantial portions of works, which should not be rekeyed without permission. It is acceptable to rekey extracts from copyright protected material under fair dealing, for criticism or review or for reporting current events, provided due acknowledgment is given.

Downloading from an online database, floppy disk or CD-ROM into a paper format
Downloading from an online database is permitted only under the terms of the licence from the database owner as part of the service contract. How much one is allowed to download is often unclear and differs from database to database, so it is impossible to give any clear advice on this. Meanwhile, the LA recommends that subscribers should study their contract for limitations on downloading (copying). However, there should not be a problem in going online and downloading the results of a search and printing it out for your personal use, as otherwise there would be no point in subscribing to the service.

The supply of a CD-ROM is determined by a contract of purchase (conditions of sale), if bought outright, or if leased, a leasing contract. CD-ROM retrieval software usually includes an option to download and this would indicate that the producer is expecting a certain amount to take place. It is advisable, however, to check the contract to determine exactly what is permissible. Generally speaking, if a CD-ROM is purchased outright and there is no relevant contractual restriction, downloading is subject to the fair dealing provisions – thus the CD-ROM would be treated as a book. It is important, therefore, to check any conditions of sale prior to purchasing a CD-ROM to see whether these conditions cover the intended use of the material. If this is not clear, then it is advisable to spell out on the order form exactly how the material will be used, thus generating your own contractual conditions. If the vendor agrees to supply the disc under those terms then there should be no other restrictions to its use.

Downloading copyright protected material from databases directly into a computer
This is only feasible if permitted by a service contract. However, many contracts forbid storing downloaded information in inhouse databases, so users who routinely download information obtained from an online database into personal bibliographical retrieval systems are often breaking their contracts, as they are storing electronic data permanently. This has been recognized by at least one database provider – DIALOG's Electronic Redistribution and Archiving system – which has introduced a scheme whereby users pay for the privilege of storing information or passing it electronically to a third party.

Sending copyright electronic material around a local area network

Networking, allowing several users access to the same commercial databases, is normally the subject of separate contractual arrangements. At present, there is no one arrangement which is acceptable to all producers. The LA is attempting to encourage standardization in this area.

Sending copyright works by fax

Although it is becoming a common form of communication, copying a copyright work and sending it by fax is still a legal grey area. Sending a copy of copyright material – for example a journal article – by fax means (a) storing it in an electronic form, and (b) making an extra hard copy to use in the machine. These are 'transient or incidental to some other use of the work' [S.17(2) & (6)] and thus infringing copyright. However, the electronic copy is unlikely to amount to a reproduction (the copy never exists in material form at any one time and at any one place as faxing involves the serial transmission of small bits of information). So, if the transmitted hard copy is destroyed and all the relevant copyright regulations have been complied with (a signed declaration has been obtained before copying), there should not be an infringing copy.

However, with the increasing sophistication of this equipment – fax modems and photocopiers with fax facilities – the recipient is now able to receive the copy in electronic form enabling storage. This is illegal and some rights owner representatives are calling for compensation for material distributed this way. The Library Association therefore suggests that unless permission has been obtained from rights owners, senders and recipients should delete the electronic version as soon as a single copy has been printed by the recipient.

The Internet (Information Superhighway)

Copyright on the Internet is a topic which causes a polarity of views. There are those who are in favour of greater restrictions, greater control and an extension of rights, and there are those that believe that copyright, as we perceive it, should be abolished and that it is irrelevant in today's technology-driven world. Many believe that copyright is already dead and that information obtained from the Internet is free of copyright restrictions. Most library and information professionals hold a more balanced view. Copyright is necessary to allow authors to control the use of their works and to provide financial incentives to create, but too much control could prevent access and stifle future creativity. (See the LA/JCC position paper *Copyright and the digital environment*, details in **Further reading list**.)

However, what appears to be free from copyright restrictions may not necessarily be so. Provided it meets the criteria for protection, a work which appears on the Internet is someone's intellectual property. It is true that at present the majority of material placed on the network is there for the express purpose of being read, copied, forwarded or downloaded. Much of it is ephemeral. But it could be dangerous to assume that permission to use or copy is given implicitly by its being available on the network. Some material may consist of infringing copies. Unless the copyright status of a work can be established and permission cleared, the LA advises that the information obtained is restricted to personal use and not re-transmitted or stored electronically for further use.

Uploading copyright protected works on to the Internet, whether to a bulletin board, web page or as part of an electronic mail message, is storing the works in electronic form, which is a restricted act and should not be done without permission or licence. Even forwarding messages received is an infringement of the sender's copyright although implicit permission is often assumed. The LA advises discretion in this practice. Some institutions have developed Codes of Practice for use of email.

Miscellaneous advice and guidance

Charging for copying

There is no requirement to levy a charge when copying under the terms of a CLA licence. There is also no requirement under the Act to charge for copies under the fair dealing provisions. Staff or students making their own copies on self-operated photocopiers under those provisions will, in many libraries, pay the cost involved either by inserting money in the machine or paying for a photocopying 'credit card'. Such charges are neither required nor prevented by the Act.

However, under the library regulations librarians are required to charge the actual cost of making copies, plus a 'contribution to the general expenses of the library'. No advice can be given as to the meaning of 'a contribution to the general expenses of the library' since it is undefined. Libraries should, however, include a reasonable amount in the charges made to users over and above the direct costs, to cover handling costs. Photocopies obtained from other libraries may be paid for by the requesting library by using BL Document Supply Centre request forms as currency. Libraries have to make their own decisions about how they effect the charging of the actual cost of making copies when obtained via interlibrary loan as the Act offers no guidance on 'charging' users directly or recharging within the library budget margins.

Some libraries offering current awareness services have introduced the device of accepting money in advance from requesting institutions and drawing from that deposit as requests are made. It is believed that this is an acceptable practice although it cannot be regarded as authorized by the Act.

Committee papers

It seems clear that multiple copies required by a committee for consideration at a meeting would not be regarded as fair dealing for 'research'. 'Private study' is clearly not applicable in the case of committees. It has been argued that 'criticism or review' is an appropriate purpose for committees. Multiple copies are allowed for this fair dealing purpose. However, the intention was probably to allow quotations to be made from published works in reviews of those works published in newspapers and magazines (see **Fair dealing: criticism or review** on p.8). It also appears that permission can only apply to copying the text rather than the typographical layout. So photocopying an extract from a report would not be allowed, although re-typing it *might* be. Similar considerations apply to fair dealing for 'news reporting'.

On the other hand, it is in the interests of the publishers and copyright owners of many documents that other organizations consider them and respond to them. This is especially so in the case of consultative documents. The following 'rules of thumb' are offered to assist in preparing committee papers:

(a) **Circular letters and similar documents seeking the views of individuals and organizations**: it may be assumed that copies may be made without permission.

(b) **Unpriced consultative documents**: if an unpriced document is labelled 'consultative' or similar, it may be assumed that the publisher wishes it to be widely circulated in order to receive comments. In most cases, it will probably be acceptable to copy for committees. Free additional copies may be easily available from the publisher, in which case this may be the preferred option.

(c) **Priced consultative documents**: it would be wise to obtain permission to copy either an extract or the whole document. An extract worth copying for a committee, e.g. the conclusions and recommendations, is likely to be considered a 'substantial' part.

(d) **Crown and Parliamentary publications** (see p.12).

(e) **All other priced publications**: it is advisable to obtain permission from the publishers.

Many publishers will freely give permission to copy for committee purposes, if asked. All copies made for committee should have a full bibliographical reference, the source of 'official' copies and should be marked 'for committee consideration only'. It cannot be assumed that committee members may make further copies to circulate in their workplace, for example. Unless specific permission has been obtained, it is advisable not to include copies of copyright documents with sets of committee papers which are sent to other people for information only. Sources of supply of the original documents may instead be included on agendas, or digests could be prepared.

Establishments covered by a CLA licence may copy copyright material covered by that licence for use by a committee within the limits of the licence.

Contents pages

The contents page of a journal counts as an article. Under the library regulations, only one article may be copied from a journal issue and then only if it has been requested by a user. The CLA licence adopts the same limitations. Therefore, copying and circulating contents pages could be seen as copyright infringement. However, it is the view of the LA that circulating journal contents pages is a way of advertising the journals and does not necessarily damage the economic rights of rights holders. In fact, the opposite damages economic rights: if users do not know what is in the journal, the journal is less likely to be read and when budgets are tight these journals are more likely to be cancelled. There are some publishers who agree with our view and do not see this practice as encouraging copyright infringement. Subscription agents are also allowing free circulation of electronic versions. However, the Publishers Association insists that unless permission is given or they are covered by a licence, contents pages must not be copied. Therefore, although the LA is unable to advise that making multiple copies of contents pages is free from the risk of prosecution, it is our view that it is unlikely that rights owners would object if a single copy of a journal contents page was displayed or circulated provided it was only to a specified group of users, (see also **Current awareness bulletins** below).

Copyright cleared work books

Some publishers allow the free copying of their works. The price of copying is incorporated into the purchase price. Copies should only be used by staff and students within the establishment.

Copying artistic works as part of a slide catalogue

Some librarians include a thumbnail print of artistic works to complement the bibliographic details of slide catalogues. Although this seems a perfectly reasonable practice, it is not without risk of accusations of copyright infringement. All slides should have been legally obtained in the first instance, i.e. purchased from a commercial source, made with permission of the copyright owner or under the terms of a licence from DACS (see p.15). If the copyright in the slides belongs to the educational establishment then there should not be a problem but other rights owners would need to be contacted for permission before copying their works. Digitizing any copyright protected work is not allowed without permission or licence as this would be storing the work in electronic form and is a restricted act. Rights owners would need to be convinced that the thumbnail copy would not be enlarged and distributed freely. Some picture libraries use black and white photographs and this is not seen to cause too many problems.

Copying by students in public libraries

Many public libraries are used by students doing research for project work as they may be more convenient than using academic libraries. Unfortunately, the CLA licence does not extend to public libraries and public librarians have to abide by the library regulations. The LA advises that public libraries and colleges cooperate on the provision of photocopies of material for group projects. Students may still copy for research and private study under fair dealing.

Copying for stock

Librarians are allowed to obtain copies from another library to place in their permanent collection (see p.9 for details). This does not mean that copies may be made from the library's own collection. Nor does it mean that copies obtained for lecturers under the library or interlibrary document supply service, or those which the lecturer makes under fair dealing, may be subsequently donated to the library as they will have been obtained and must be used for the purposes of research or private study only. Copies required for library stock under **S.41** may be obtained from the BLDSC using a special form for this purpose. Copies legitimately obtained for stock may be copied further under the terms of the CLA licence. This does not apply to copies obtained under the BL copyright cleared service. See also **Short loan and reserve collections** on p.25.

Copying for the visually impaired

Rights holders are usually sympathetic to the needs of the visually impaired. However, in order to reproduce a document in Braille, on tape, or in a large print version, permission must be obtained first.

The Music Publishers Association has recognized the needs of the partially sighted by giving permission to make large print versions of printed music subject to certain conditions. Before making the copy, the publisher of the original text must be contacted first for approval. The conditions are: that the music was legitimately obtained; that multiple copies are not made; and that the enlarged copies are not re-sold. If all these conditions are met to the satisfaction of the publisher, applicants will be provided with a sticker to place on the large print version verifying its legitimacy, see *Music in large print*. RNIB/Music Publishers' Association, 1994 (for details see **Further reading list**).

Copying from newspapers

Copying articles from newspapers is no different from copying from journals so, for research and private study purposes, apply the same limits. Many newspaper publishers including local publishers have allowed copying for educational purposes, so multiple copying of several items may be allowed. It is essential, however, that permission (preferably in writing) is obtained first. However, a licence for multiple copying is now available from the Newspaper Licensing Agency, see p.16.

Newspaper publishers, apart from *The Independent*, have not mandated the Copyright Licensing Agency to use their material, although it is believed that negotiations are taking place. *The Times Educational Supplement* is defined as a periodical and so copying extracts comes under the terms of the CLA licence.

Current awareness bulletins

Anyone may produce an in-house current awareness bulletin if the bibliographic details have been input manually i.e. not obtained by photocopying contents pages or downloaded from an online database. Own annotations may be included, and **S.60** allows any abstracts published along with articles in scientific or technical journals to be incorporated in a current awareness bulletin either by photocopying or re-keying, unless a licensing scheme becomes available to cover the copying of such abstracts. (There is no licensing scheme at present for abstracts.) The interpretation of 'scientific' or 'technical' may be assumed to be broad.

The Act clearly authorizes non-profit based libraries to provide a copying service to any member of the public in response to requests. However any library which advertised a copying service in direct association with a bulletin, especially if distributed beyond the normal clientele or catchment area, could be considered to be soliciting requests rather than responding to them. Such services could damage rights-owner markets because local demand for the original media concerned might be reduced if reliance is placed on current awareness and copying. Therefore, The Library Association recommends that any library sending bulletin copies outside its own clientele or catchment area should include the following statement:

> Those wishing to obtain copies of items in this issue should consult their own (or 'local') libraries.

It is also preferable to include standard declaration forms only in issues distributed to the library's own clientele. If forms are included in all copies it should be made clear that they are for use only by registered members in the relevant catchment area or 'closed' clientele.

It is an infringement to make multiple copies of relevant journal articles as part of an SDI service and disseminate them to users. Contents pages are covered by copyright in the same way as other items in journals (see also **Contents pages** on p.21).

Damaged tapes

There is no provision in the Act for making back-up copies of commercially produced sound recordings or videos. A damaged tape beyond repair which is still required for loan would have to be discarded and another purchased. If the material is no longer available for purchase, a copy may be made from another source (see **Copying for replacement** on p.10) but under this regulation the replacement copy has to be for reference only.

Declaration forms

Signed declaration forms should be kept by the library which is making the copies as this would be part of the evidence if a case of alleged copyright infringement was brought against the library. For legislative purposes these forms should be kept for six years after the end of the year the copying took place, because an action under the legislation may be made at any time until six years after the alleged infringement occurred. There is nothing in the Act to suggest in what order they should be kept.

The Library Association has been advised that sending a photocopy declaration form by fax is acceptable. Where fax copies are on non-permanent paper, originals will still be needed for record keeping. At present, electronic signatures are not recognized under UK law.

Exhibitions

Artistic works may be displayed or exhibited without permission because this does not infringe copyright.

Foreign material

All material from countries party to the Berne Convention (a few countries do not belong) should be given the same protection as UK material. Similarly, UK works are protected under the copyright laws of other Berne member states. However, the extension of the term of protection in EU member states for literary, dramatic, musical and artistic works from 50 to 70 years has meant that non EEA material will only be protected for the Berne minimum – 50 years. Some works in France have an extra nine years' protection to compensate authors for the period lost in the two World Wars. The UK does not recognize this extra term so French works have the same protection as other EEA member states.

Free material

Material which is circulated free of charge – annual reports, brochures, leaflets etc. – is still protected by copyright. Only copy in multiple with permission or obtain further copies.

Market research reports

Because the publishers of these reports (e.g. Mintel) invest a lot of time and money in their production, they try to forbid any copying from them. However, unless they have been purchased on the understanding that the library will prevent any copying taking place (i.e. the library has contracted with the publisher), copying for purposes allowed in the Act is still permissible. Discretion should be used in deciding a fair amount to be copied for research or private study as each report may be considered a whole work in itself, and it is advisable, where possible, to copy for students under the library regulations using the declaration form. See also advice on **Prohibitive statements** on p.24.

Microforms

Microforms which reproduce an original work without amendment (for example, a microfilmed report) should be treated in the same way as the original. The microform is a copyright photograph but with only a facsimile copy of works on it, and copies have no copyright in themselves. A microform publisher might own additional rights as editor or compiler of an anthology, in which case permission to copy may be necessary. Otherwise only the rights of the authors and publishers of the original works apply to ordinary sized copying.

Mixed media packages

Each component has its own copyright but the publisher may make a blanket claim on the format of the package. Copying is restricted to the terms of the package deal but remember also that copying from anything other than printed material would be an infringement.

Permission

If, when seeking permission to copy, it proves impossible to trace the rights owner and there is evidence that reasonable enquiry has been made, copying could take place. What constitutes *reasonable enquiry* would have to be decided in a court of law if the rightful owner chose to prosecute. The standards of conduct expected by the law for information professionals is likely to be higher than that for the ordinary member of the public. Accordingly, in ascertaining whether or not a work is truly anonymous, that copyright has expired, or that the author of a work has died, information professionals would be expected to be aware of and make full use of all sources of information appropriate to the nature of the rights required. Enquiries should be tempered by economic realities, and should be measured against the expected or probable value of the use envisaged by the person or organization wishing to make use of a work of undetermined copyright status. Prosecutions for infringement can take place up six years after the year of an alleged offence, so records of steps taken should be kept for seven years.

Photographs

There is no restriction on the performance or showing of artistic works, including photographs (see also p.23). Note that photographers have a legal right to have a reasonably prominent credit whenever a work is published, exhibited or shown in a film or on television. This right does not apply to employees who take photographs under contract of employment, unless the employer allows them to retain their rights.

Establishing whether an old photograph is out of copyright can be difficult and the problem is exacerbated by some confusion over the length of the copyright term. As from January 1996 in the UK, it is believed that photographs created before 1 August 1989 are now protected for 70 calendar years from when the negative was taken, unless subject to Crown or international organizations' copyright. If Crown copyright applies, protection is for only 50 calendar years from the date of taking. If that of international organizations, it is never less than 50 calendar years, but may be greater. It will be necessary to check this in particular cases. It is no longer true to say that all photographs taken prior to 1934 are out of copyright since many of them are now the subject of revived rights, although determining who, if anyone, now owns the rights, is a specialist problem. The original rights holder would be *the person who owned the film when the photograph was taken* unless Crown copyright applies. This wording causes great difficulty when trying to determine the rights holder because it implies that ownership is defined in terms of a natural *person*, not a legal one such as a company or other form of corporate body, who were and usually are the owners of this kind of intellectual property.

Copyright in unpublished photographs is the same for all unpublished works: 50 years from the end of 1989 (the year the 1988 Act became law) i.e. 2039.

A useful little guide, although it will now need updating, is *The ABC of photographic copyright* published by the British Photographers' Liaison Committee (see Appendix C for details).

Playing music in educational establishments

Playing music, other than to an audience of teachers and students, counts as a 'public performance' and will need to be licensed. For example, aerobics classes for people not registered as students or employees of an institution would almost certainly constitute a public performance. Phonographic Performance Ltd (PPL) controls the public performance and broadcasting of its members' sound recordings. Members of PPL consist of most of the well known recording companies, multinationals and independents as well as a number of specialized repertoire producers. The Performing Right Society (PRS) controls the licensing for use of the composers' and music publishers' rights. So any college or university considering playing a sound recording in public may need a licence from both PPL and the PRS. Any establishment considering giving a concert of live music only, i.e. not using sound recordings, may need to have a licence from the PRS only. The costs for a one-off event are likely to be very modest. The

PPL and the PRS will be pleased to discuss individual needs. PPL provides a very useful information sheet. Contact PPL or the PRS (details in Appendix C).

Profit basis

The Act's phrase 'established or conducted for profit' applies to the parent organizations as well as to the services themselves, but the term is not defined. It seems reasonable to assume that it means that the organization or service concerned has the objective of attaining an excess of income over expenditure. The mere selling of services to recover a proportion of the expenditure, or even all the direct costs, without covering overheads and without making a true surplus would not be construed as 'established or conducted for profit'. If a service were split off as an independent business without subsidy, it would then become 'established or conducted for profit'.

Prohibitive statements

Many publications contain statements which seem to forbid any copying or lending. By purchasing them for the library, it could be said that librarians had entered into an 'implied contract' with the publishers. Where copying is permitted by the Act (e.g. under fair dealing or the library regulations) or under a licence, it is most unlikely that a rights owner would bring a claim of infringement of 'implied contract' to court because of some phrase which had been put on an item. The law on unfair contract terms could be used in defence in any case, should a need arise. In general, therefore, it is advised that prohibitive or restrictive phrases, which seek to limit copying or use of an item to a greater extent than statute, may be ignored. Only if conditions of sale were agreed or a full contract were entered into could a rights owner have a sound case on contractual grounds. Contract law can override statute law in such circumstances.

Those worried about conditions of sale and wishing to be safe, could put standard phrases of their own on order forms, indicating that the item is required for a library and will be treated like the rest of the stock in accordance with statute, thus generating their own contractual arrangements. This advice also applies to the purchase of videos, sound recordings, CD-ROMs and open learning material for lending for educational purposes.

Self-service photocopiers and liability

The responsibility for any photocopying machine within the library premises rests with the librarian. Any infringement which occurs on such machines could therefore involve the library staff and the educational establishment if a case were brought to court. It is important, therefore, that every effort is made to instil respect and compliance for copyright in staff and other users. It is the LA's view that self-operated photocopiers may continue to be housed in libraries, provided that:

- prominent notices are displayed alongside the photocopiers in a position such that users will find them difficult to ignore. The notices should make it clear that copyright is protected by law; what limits may be applied; and should advise users to ask staff for guidance when in doubt. (Laminated posters can be obtained from LAHQ, see p.28 for details);
- similar information is incorporated in publicity material or library user guides and in the library's regulations;
- user education and induction programmes also cover copyright;
- library staff training programmes include copyright so that appropriate advice can be given to users; line managers responsible for library resources should be included in such programmes.

Management should also consider cautionary statements in staff conditions of service and library conditions of access. It is a matter of internal policy whether library staff should intervene if they observe apparent infringements but the view of the LA is that the appropriate member(s) of staff should be informed. The ultimate responsibility rests with the Vice-Chancellor or College Principal who is responsible for the actions of employees. However, the CLA licence does provide indemnity for copying as part of compliance with its terms.

Short loan and reserve collections

Institutions with a CLA licence may make copies of extracts of material already in stock for short loan collections, observing the terms of the licence, which also permits the further copying of such items by users, sometimes called 'cascade' or 'systematic single copying'.

The LA believes that the OS and BSI licences for multiple copying also may be taken to include copying for short loan stock.

Academic libraries are entitled to put into stock single copies of items obtained from another prescribed library under **S.41** provisions. (See **Interlibrary copying for stock** p.9.) The CLA licence permits futher copies to be made for stock, and 'cascade' copying by users.

Copyright-cleared copies acquired from BLDSC or other licensed sources may also be stocked, but in this instance, no subsequent copying by users is permitted. Despite warning notices, it is difficult to see how this ban could be enforced. The LA recommends, as good practice, the clear display of full bibliographic details in a prominent position, together with a clear warning whenever further copying is not permitted.

Some institutions have chosen to make and put into stock a limited number of study packs. A prohibition on further copying is a condition of permission granted by CLARCS in these cases.

Theses and dissertations

These are unpublished works and how they are treated depends on whether the copyright belongs to the student or has been assigned to the university. In many universities, the student is either obliged or voluntarily deposits a copy of the thesis in the library. Strictly speaking, permission to access and/or copy these works should be obtained from the author before it is deposited in the library and this should preferably be done before the student leaves. If the student has not prohibited the copying, it is advised that the conditions for library copying of unpublished works (see below) should be followed rather than copying under fair dealing as this does give some control over possible copyright infringement or plagiarism. If the university holds the copyright then it is a matter of internal policy about how such works are treated. Most universities have strict rules of access to such works.

Translations

Translating a whole work means making an adaptation which is an infringement [S.21(3)(a)(i)]. Permission has to be sought from the author. If permission is granted, then the copyright in the new work belongs to the translator although the original copyright stays with the author.

If a user wishes to translate any copyright work, even for research or private study purposes, the copyright owner must be consulted. This is not only because of the requirement for permission under **S.21(3)(a)(i)**, but also because of the author's moral rights [**SS.77–89**] which imply that the author should be made aware of a risk of misinterpretation.

Unpublished works

Unpublished manuscripts are copyright only until 70 years from the death of the author [**S.12**], not in perpetuity (or until publication) as in previous legislation. Note, however, that material already in copyright when the Act came into force (i.e. works by an author who died before August 1989) remain in copyright until 1 January 2040. [**Sch.1 S.12(4)**]. Please refer also to advice on **Photographs** on p.23.

Videos

Provided it is for instructional purposes, the Act allows commercially produced videos to be shown in educational establishments. So phrases such as 'licensed for home use only' or 'may not be performed in clubs, prisons or schools' may be ignored as long as the audience consists of students and those giving instruction only.

There is also no restriction on the lending of these videos either, provided the service is not run on a commercial basis, but it is advisable to make it clear when ordering that the intention is to lend (follow advice given on **Prohibitive statements** on p.24).

Whole works

Strictly speaking, whole works may not be copied without permission as they constitute a substantial amount. Examples of whole works include: poems, signed encyclopaedia articles (although it may be possible to copy extracts from unsigned ones), journal contents pages, indexes, knitting patterns, examination papers.

Works created under the terms of an employment contract

In general, the creator of a work owns the copyright but the Act lays down that ownership of copyright in a work created *in the course of employment* belongs to the employer. Some institutions have chosen to distinguish in contracts of employment between material created directly for teaching i.e. pathway or course documentation, and scholarly activity such as journal articles or books, There is much variation among HE institutions in this respect.

Current debate about the terms under which HE and FE institutions purchase licences to permit the use of copyright material is prompting fundamental reconsideration of the ownership of copyright works created by teaching staff in the employment of Universities and Colleges.

Case law

This section has been included to give a selection of some of the relevant copyright case law. Interesting foreign cases have also been included.

Artistic works

The Design and Artists Copyright Society (DACS) sued art publishers Thames and Hudson for failing to pay royalties for the reproduction and paintings belonging to the estate of the German painter Max Beckmann. DACS said they were trying to bring royalties in line with those for authors, film-makers and musicians. As a defence, the publishers claimed fair dealing for criticism and review and argued that having to pay royalties would double the price of art books. The DACS case collapsed, however, when Christiane Beckmann, the artist's granddaughter, failed to testify.

■ **Copyright threat to modern art books: fears grow that royalty payments will raise prices.** *The Sunday Telegraph* 26 February 1995.

■ **Royalties victory for art publisher.** *The Sunday Telegraph* 19 March 1995.

Artistic works: maps

In March 1995, Ordnance Survey successfully prosecuted two publishing companies, Streetwise Map and Guide Ltd, Norfolk and Color Maps International, Norwich for copying OS maps and incorporating them in their publications without licence.

■ *OS press release* 5 June 1995.

Artistic works: photographs

A Belfast photographer sued publisher Vermilion (part of Random House) for infringement of his copyright and moral right of integrity after his award winning Time for Peace photograph was manipulated and used on the cover of a recipe book *Recipes for peace*, without permission.

■ **Look what they've done to my photo!** *Journalist Weekly* 16 October 1995.

An ex-Mayor of Tower Hamlets was fined and ordered to pay compensation costs to the photographer for illegally using his photograph in a political leaflet. The photograph had been lifted deliberately from a copy of the *London Daily News* and used to smear an opponent.

■ **Former Mayor fined for copyright breach.** *British journal of photography* Vol. 138 No. 6843. 24 October 1991.

■ **Ex Mayor of Tower Hamlets convicted over 'political smear' leaflet.** Press release from *Stephens Innocent* 16 October 1991.

Books and periodicals

Publishers Schofield and Sims, the owners of copyright in certain mathematics textbooks, claimed damages from the Forest of Dean Council for infringement of copyright by Royal Forest of Dean College. The college was alleged to have made multiple copies from these books at a time when the County Council did not have a licence from the publishers to do so.

■ **School book rumpus.** *Gloucester Citizen* 10 September 1990.

Publishers in the US (American Geophysical Union, Elsevier Science, Pergamon, Springer, Wiley and Academic Press) successfully sued Texaco for photocopying from their books and journals for their staff without permission. In the decision ruled in July 1992, despite the claim by Texaco that they were copying under fair use, the judge ruled that companies cannot copy articles for internal use without first obtaining permission and compensating the rights holders. An appeal was lodged in September 1992 but the ruling was upheld.

■ **Appeals Court upholds Texaco copyright ruling.** *Bookseller* 11 November 1994.

Note: The US *fair use* is not quite the same as the UK's fair dealing but, nevertheless, this is an important precedent with implications for profit-based organizations.

In the case brought against Kinko's Graphic Corporation, a nationwide chain of photocopying stores in the USA, it was ruled that Kinko's infringed publishers' (Basic Books, HarperCollins, John Wiley & Sons, McGraw-Hill, Penguin USA, Prentice Hall, Richard D. Irwin & William Morrow) copyrights by reproducing excerpts from books and selling them in anthologies for college students. Kinko's claim was that the photocopying was necessary for educational purposes and used fair use as a defence. This was ruled out by the judge who maintained that the real purpose for copying was for commercial reasons as a large portion of their earnings came from photocopying substantial portions of copyrighted material.

■ **Photocopying chain found in violation of copyright law.** *The Chronicle of Higher Education* 3 April 1991.

The Copyright Licensing Agency, acting on behalf of publishers, the Open University and Centaur Press, obtained a considerable financial settlement for unauthorized photocopying from Essenheath Ltd – the commercial arm of Greenwich College, an independent business college in London. The CLA hired a private investigator to enrol as a student and found evidence that the college had reproduced copyright material without permission or licence for use in course work by students. The college was ordered to take out a CLA licence.

In 1984 Manchester City Council was ordered to pay £75,000 for copyright infringement. The case was triggered by a supply teacher who was astonished to find quantities of his own book in photocopied form in a school stock room.

■ **Private investigator helps CLA win settlement.** *Bookseller* 5 March 1993.

■ **In the twilight world of the copyright busters: Jonathan Croall reports on moves to crack down on illegal photocopying.** *Guardian Education* 16 March 1993.

A Dallas Federal Judge banned Enmark Gas Corp., a gas based distributor, from 'cover to cover photocopying and facsimile transmission' of *Gas Daily*, a newsletter publication. Enmark had copied the newsletter and distributed copies to employees without permission. The company was unaware that its actions were improper.

■ **Federal Judge bans copying.** *Wall Street Journal* 12 March 1992.

In September 1994, The Copyright Agency Ltd, (the Australian CLA) acting on behalf of 12 academic publishers in Australia, a case was brought against Victorian University of Technology for the practice of compiling course anthologies for students. The court in Sydney dismissed the case but the decision has since been overturned on appeal.

■ **VUT in court to defend textbook photocopying.** *Australian* 7 September 1994.

■ **Ruling will prove a death sentence to our wordsmiths.** *Australian* 9th November 1994.

Computer software

In the USA, Lotus Development sued Borland International in 1990 for including a menu system in its Quattro Pro spreadsheet similar to the one in Lotus 1-2-3. After a lengthy trial, the US Supreme Court concluded that the menu structure of the Lotus program 'is uncopyrightable' and is merely a 'method of operation'. (This case is still in dispute).

■ **Judge delivers copyright blow.** *Computing* 28 May 1992.

■ **High Court to hear Lotus-Borland copyright dispute.** *Newsbytes News Network Predicasts PROMPT* 28 September 1995.

Another similar dispute is between Apple Computer which sued Microsoft and Hewlett Packard for allegedly copying its Macintosh user interface. Apple claimed that Microsoft and HP infringed the look and feel of its graphical user interface (GUI). The Northern California judge threw out the case.

■ **Apple emerges as a winner against Microsoft in copyright battle.** *COMPUTING Reuter Textline* 30 April 1992.

■ **Judge throws out Apple's GUI suit.** *Infoworld* ABI-INFORM 7 June 1993.

Following proceedings against the London Borough of Greenwich by the Federation Against Software Theft and the Business Software alliance on behalf of Lotus and Xtree, an out-of-court settlement was agreed. Illegal software was found in the Housing Directorate.

■ **Greenwich faces FAST software theft charge.** *Computer weekly* 12 December 1991.

■ **London Borough of Greenwich and software publishers agree out of court settlement in software copying case.** *Greenwich Council press release* 10 January 1992.

Note: major software development companies are increasingly concerned about illegal copies of their software which are being made and distributed to large companies and so defrauding them of large sums of revenue. They estimate that 'piracy' is costing their industry millions of pounds per annum. FAST – Federation Against Software Theft – was formed to combat this piracy. Without prior warning, premises which are suspected of holding or using illegal software can be raided. Criminal proceedings can be started leading to hefty damages. Several companies have been prosecuted successfully.

Music

The Royal Ulster Constabulary Male Voice Choir had to pay £2,000 damages and costs to the Music Publishers' Association for photocopying scores.

■ **Not so happy.** *Independent* 13 June 1992.

Videos

An English language school in York illicitly copied 300 videos. The school paid £71,000 in an out-of-court settlement.

■ **In the twilight world of the copyright busters:**

Jonathan Croall reports on moves to crack down on illegal photocopying. *Guardian Education* 16 March 1993.

Performance right

A cinema manageress was convicted of copyright infringement for screening Stanley Kubrick's film *A clockwork orange* in Britain. The film had been banned by Kubrick himself who was exercising his moral right of disclosure. The case was brought by the Federation Against Copyright Theft (FACT). The film used was a pirated video.

■ **Cinema boss accused over Clockwork Orange showing.** *Daily Telegraph* 5 February 1993.

■ **Clockwork Orange woman pays £1000: Kubrick's banned film depicting teenage violence returns after 20 years to spark fresh controversy.** *The Daily Telegraph* 24 March 1993.

■ **Kubrick screening breached copyright.** *The Guardian* 24 March 1993.

Rental right

The British Phonographic Industry was granted an injunction to prevent an Eastbourne store, Satin Sounds, from renting out CDs and music videos.

■ **Trade faces the music.** *Video business* February 9 1991.

Electronic copyright

Jonathan Tasini, President of the New York based National Writers Union, and nine other writers sued database operators: Mead Data Central (owned by Reed Elsevier) and three major publishers: The New York Times Corporation, The Times-Mirror Corporation, and the Time Warner Corporation, for using their articles in an online database without permission or payment. The National Union of Journalists is also concerned about a number of UK publishers who put their work online without permission or payment.

■ **Copyright reservations.** *The Guardian* 8 June 1995.

Posters

The Library Association produces an attractive A3 size laminated poster 'Before You Copy Read This' intended for display beside photocopying machines. The costs per copy are: £2.50 (non-members £3.50) for up to four copies; £2.00 (£3.00 non-members) for 5–10; and £1.50 (£2.50 non-members) for 11 or more. Payment may be made by sending a cheque with order or if that is not convenient a pro-forma invoice may be sent on receipt of an order. Cheques should be made payable to The Library Association. Orders should be sent to: COPYRIGHT POSTERS, Information Services, The Library Association, 7 Ridgmount Street, London WC1E 7AE. It would also be helpful if an adhesive self-addressed label could be sent with orders.

Other LA guides

In addition to this guide, The Library Association has produced the following (available from Library Association Publishing):

Copyright in industrial and commercial libraries
Copyright in health libraries
Copyright in public libraries
Copyright in school libraries
Copyright in voluntary sector libraries

LA/JCC Working Party on Copyright

This Working Party is a merger of the LA Sub-committee on Copyright and the Joint Consultative Committee's (JCC) Sub-committee on Copyright representing the members of the following organizations: Aslib (the Association for Information Management), the Institute of Information Scientists, The Library Association, SCONUL (Standing Conference of National and University Libraries) and the Society of Archivists. It is the main voice speaking on copyright on behalf of the library and information profession. The Working Party is concerned that the economic rights of creators and information providers are balanced with the needs of library and information staff and their users to gain access to information.

Appendix A: Prescribed libraries and archives

1. **Public libraries**
   Any library administered by :
   - (a) public library authority in England and Wales
   - (b) a statutory library authority in Scotland
   - (c) an Education and Library Board in Northern Ireland

2. **National Libraries**
   British Library
   National Library of Wales
   National Library of Scotland
   Bodleian Library, Oxford
   University Library, Cambridge.

3. **Libraries in educational establishments**
   A library of a school
   Libraries of universities which are empowered to award degrees
   Libraries of institutions providing further or higher education.

4. **Parliamentary and government libraries**

5. **Local Government Libraries**
   Any library administered by:
   - (a) A local authority in England and Wales
   - (b) A local authority in Scotland
   - (c) A district council in Northern Ireland

6. **Other libraries**
   Any library which encourages the study of bibliography, education, fine arts, history, languages, law, literature, medicine, music, philosophy, religion, science (including natural and social science) or technology.
   Any library outside the UK which encourages the study of the above subjects.

Source: SI 1989:1068 and SI 1989:1212

Appendix B: Prescribed copyright declaration form

DECLARATION: COPY OF ARTICLE OR PART OF PUBLISHED WORK*

To:

    The Librarian of ....Library

    [Address of Library]

Please supply me with a copy of:

    [1]the article in the periodical, the particulars of which are [   ]

    [1]the part of the published work, the particulars of which are [   ]

required by me for the purposes of research or private study.

I declare that –

    (a) I have not previously been supplied with a copy of the same material by you
           or any other librarian;

    (b) I will not use the copy except for research or private study and will not supply a copy of
           it to any other person; and

    (c) to the best of my knowledge no other person with whom I work or study has made or
           intends to make, at or about the same time as this request, a request for substantially
           the same material for substantially the same purpose.

I understand that if the declaration is false in a material particular the copy supplied to me
by you will be an infringing copy and that I shall be liable for infringement of copyright as if I
had made the copy myself.

                                                               Signature[2] ....
                                                               Date..

Name ....

Address ....

        ....

        ....

[1] Delete whichever is inappropriate.

[2] This must be the personal signature of the person making the request. A stamped or typewritten signature, or the signature of an agent, is NOT acceptable.

* A similar declaration form for unpublished works is also to be found in SI 1989:1212

Appendix C: List of useful addresses

The British Copyright Council, 29 Berners Street, London W1P 4AA
Tel: 0171 359 1895

The British Photographers' Liaison Committee (incorporating The Committee on Photographic Copyright) 9–10 Domingo Street. London EC1 0TA
Tel: 0171 608 1441

British Standards Institution, 389 Chiswick High Road, London W4 4AL
Tel: 0181 996 9000

BT Group Legal Services, Intellectual Property Department, 120 Holborn, London EC1N 2TE
Tel: 0171 492 8139

Copyright Licensing Agency, 90 Tottenham Court Road, London W1P 9HE
Tel:0171 436 5931

Department of Trade & Industry Intellectual Property & Policy Directorate, Hazlitt House, 45 Southampton Buildings, London WC2A 1AR
Tel: 0171 438 4777

Design and Artists Copyright Society, Parchment House, 13 Northburgh Street, London EC1V 0AH
Tel: 0171 336 8811

Educational Recording Agency, ISIS House, 74 New Oxford Street, London WC1A 1EF
Tel: 0171 436 4883

HMSO, Copyright Unit, St Clements House, Colegate, Norwich NR3 1BQ
Tel: 01603 621000

The Library Association, 7 Ridgmount Street, London WC1E 7AE
Tel: 0171 636 7543

The LA/JCC Working Party on Copyright, c/o The Library Association (as above)

Music Publishers' Association Ltd, 3rd Floor, Strand Gate, 18–20 York Buildings, London WC2N 6JU
Tel: 0171 839 7779

Newspaper Licensing Agency Ltd, 17 Lyons Crescent, Tonbridge, Kent TN19 1EX
Tel: 01732 360333

Open University Educational Enterprises Ltd, 12 Cofferidge Close, Stony Stratford, Milton Keynes MK11 1BY
Tel: 01908 261662

Ordnance Survey, Copyright Branch, Romsey Road, Maybush, Southampton SO9 4DH
Tel: 01703 792706

Performing Right Society, 29–33 Berners Street, London W1P 4AA
Tel: 0171 580 5544

Phonographic Performance Ltd, Ganton House, 14–22 Ganton Street, London W1V 1LB
Tel: 0171 437 0311

Video Performance Ltd, Ganton House, 14–22 Ganton Street, London W1V 1LB
Tel: 0171 437 0311

The Act and relevant Statutory Instruments

Copyright, Designs and Patents Act 1988 London, HMSO. ISBN 0 10 544888 5 Price: £12.50

The Copyright (Certification of Licensing Scheme for Educational Recording of Broadcasts) (Guild Sound and Vision Limited) Order 1990. SI 1990:878. HMSO. ISBN 0 11 003878 9 Price: £1.70.

The Copyright (Certification of Licensing Scheme for Educational Recording of Broadcasts and Cable Programmes) (Educational Recording Agency Limited) Order 1990. SI 1990:879. HMSO. ISBN 0 11 003878 7 Price: £0.95.

The Copyright (Computer Programs) Regulations 1992. SI 1992:3233. HMSO. ISBN 0 11 025116 4 Price: £1.50.

The Copyright (Educational Establishments) (No 2) Order 1989. SI 1990:1068. HMSO. ISBN 0 11 097068 3 Price: £0.50.

The Copyright (Librarians and Archivists) (Copying of Copyright Material) Regulations 1989 SI 1989:1212. HMSO. ISBN 0 11 097212 0 Price: £1.65.

The Duration of Copyright and Rights in Performances Regulations 1995 SI 1995:3297. HMSO. ISBN 0 11 053833 1 Price: £3.70.

Further reading list

(Note: because of the recent changes in copyright legislation, most of the publications given below will need to be revised.)

The ABC of UK photographic copyright. British Photographers Liaison Committee, 1994. ISBN 0 9514671 1 5.

Copyright in multimedia: Papers from the Aslib conference held on 18 and 19 July 1995. Aslib, 1995. ISBN 0 85142 359 0.

CORNISH, GRAHAM P. *Copyright: interpreting the law for librarians.* Library Association Publishing, 1990. ISBN 0 85365 709 2 (a new edition is expected in late 1996).

DE FREITAS, Denis. *The law of copyright and rights in performances.* British Copyright Council, 1990. ISBN 0 901737 05 4.

LA/JCC Working Party on Copyright. *Copyright and the digital environment,* 1995 (position paper available from Information Services at the LA).

Music in large print. RNIB/Music Publishers' Association, 1994. ISBN 185878 026 8.

PHILLIPS, Jeremy, Wall, Raymond and Oppenheim, Charles. *Aslib guide to copyright.* Aslib, 1994. ISBN 0 851 42 311 6 (Loose-leaf, available on subscription.)

PHILLIPS, Jeremy, Durie, Robyn and Karet, Ian. *Whale on copyright.* 4th ed. Sweet & Maxwell, 1993. ISBN 0 421 45210 2.

POST, J. B. and Foster, M. R. *Copyright: a handbook for archivists.* Society of Archivists, 1992. ISBN 0 902 886 43 6.

WALL, Raymond A. *Copyright made easier.* Aslib, 1993. ISBN 0 85142 310 8.

Index

abstracts 11. 22
adaptation
  computer program 17
  subtitling 11
  translation 25
Academic Press 16
adaptation right 7
aerial photographs 13
aerobics classes 24
annual reports 23
anonymous works 11
anthologies 12
arbitration
  Copyright Tribunal 14
articles 11, 22
artistic works 6, 13, 21, 23
  advertising for sale 11
  case law 26
  fair dealing: criticism or review 8
  incidental inclusion 8
  term of protection 7
ARLIS 15
Aslib 15
assignment of copyright 6
Association for Colleges 14
audiovisual material
  copying for instruction 10
Authors' Licensing and Collecting Society 14

back-up copy 17
Berne Convention 8, 23
bibliographical retrieval systems 19
Blackwell Publishers 16
Braille 22
BRICMICS 13
British Library 15, 20, 22
British Standards 12, 16, 25
broadcasting right 7
broadcasts 6
  free public showing 11
  term of protection 6
brochures 23
bulletin board 20

cable programme services 6
  term of protection 7
cable programmes 6
  free public showing 11
cascade copying 25
catalogue slide 21
CD-ROMs 12, 18, 19, 24
  downloading 19

charging for copying 9, 20
circular letters 21
CLA see Copyright Licensing Agency
CLARCS 14, 25
clip art 19
clubs
  playing sound recordings 11
College Employers Forum 14
commercial rental 16
commercial research 9
Commitee of Vice-Chancellors and Principals 14
committees 21
compilation 6, 18
computer generated works 6
computer programs 6, 19
  EU Directive 17
computer software
  case law 27
concerts 24
conditions of sale see purchasing contract
conference proceedings 14
consultative documents 21
contents pages 21, 26
copy shops 26
copying limits 11
copyright cleared service 21, 25
  British Library 15
Copyright Licensing Agency 14, 20, 21, 22, 25
  case law 27
copyright owners 6
Copyright Tribunal 14, 17
criticism 8, 20, 21
Crown copyright 6
  photographs 23
Crown publications 12
current awareness bulletins 22
current events 8, 19

DACS see Design and Artists Copyright Society
damaged items 10, 23
databases 6, 17
dealing 8
declaration forms 9, 23
  sending by fax 23
decompilation 17
derogatory treatment see integrity right
Design and Artists Copyright Society 15, 26
DIALOG 19
digital mapping 13
disclosure right 7
display 23
dissemination 18
dissertations 25
document image processor see scanners
document supply 8

downloading 18, 19
dramatic works 6
    performance 10
    term of protection 6
duration of term 24
    EU Directive 17

EDINA16
educational copying 10
Educational Recording Agency 15
electrocopying 18, 28
electronic mail 18, 20
Electronic Redistribution and Archiving *see*
    DIALOG
electronic signatures 23
electronic storage 7, 19, 20
e-mail *see* electronic mail
employment contract 6, 24, 26
encyclopaedias 18, 26
ERA *see* Educational Recording Agency
examination papers 7, 26
examinations 7, 10
excluded categories of works 15
exhibitions 23
extended copyright 17, 19

FACT *see* Federation Against Copyright Theft
fair dealing 8, 19
false attribution 7
FAST *see* Federation Against Software Theft
fax 18, 20
Federation Against Copyright Theft 28
Federation Against Software Theft 27
films 6
    term of protection 6
    incidental inclusion 8
    performance 10
floppy disk 19
foreign material 23
free material 23
French copyright 23
further education licence 14

Goad plans 13

Hansard 12
higher education licence 14
HMSO 12

illustrations 13
importing works 7
incidental inclusion 8
indexes 26
Information Superhighway 20
infringement 7

Institute of Information Scientists 15, 28
Institute of Physics Publishing 16
instruction 10
integrity right 7, 19
interlibrary document supply 9, 20, 22
international organizations 6
international transfer of works 18
Internet 20

judicial proceedings 11

knitting patterns 26

LA/JCC Working Party on Copyright 28
leaflets 23
liability 8, 24
Library Association 15, 18, 28
library regulations 8, 9
licensing 14
literary works 6
    term of protection 6
local area network 18, 20

manipulation 19
mapping 13, 16
maps
    case law 26
market research reports 23
microforms 23
Mintel 23
mixed media 23
moral rights 7
    EU Directive 17
    violation 19
multimedia 18
multiple copying 8
    criticism or review 8
    research or private study 11
music 14, 24
    case law 27
Music Publishers' Association 22
musical works 6
    term of protection 6

National Subtitling Library for Deaf People 11
networking 18, 20
news reporting 8
newspaper copying 16, 22
Newspaper Licensing Agency 16, 22

off-air recording 10, 11, 15, 18
Official Journal of the EU 13
online databases 18; *see also* databases
    case law 28
    downloading 19

term of protection 6
open learning material 16
Open University 15
optical scanner *see* scanners
Ordnance Survey 13, 25
    licensing 15
out-of-print item 10

pamphlets 12
Parliamentary copyright 6
Parliamentary proceedings 11, 12
paternity right 7
penalties for infringement 8
performance rights 7
    case law 28
Performing Right Society 24
periodicals 11
permission to copy 21, 23
Phonographic Performance Ltd 24
photocopiers 24, 25
photograph of television broadcast 11
photographs 13, 22, 23
    case law 26
    disclosure right 8
    news reporting 8
    term of protection 6
piracy 19, 27
plagiarism 19
poems 12
posters 28
    photocopier 25
premises, used for performance 7
prescribed libraries 9
press releases 12
private copying
    EU Directive 16, 17
private study 8, 21
profit basis 24
prohibitive statements 24
protection of databases 24
    EU Directive 17
public domain 19
public inspection 11
public lending 16, 17
public performance 7, 24
publication right 7, 17
publicity material 25
published editions 6
Publishers Association 21
Publishers' Licensing Society 14
purchasing contracts 19
    prohibitive statements 24

quotations 8

radio *see* off-air recording
reading in public 11
reasonable enquiry 23
recording equipment levy 18
rekeying 18, 19
remuneration of authors 17
rental and lending right
    EU Directive 17
rental right 16
    case law 28
replacement copying 10
reports 7, 12
reproduction right 7
reprographic process 10
research 8
reserve collections 25
review 8, 21
revived copyright 17
rights owners 6
Royal Commission 11

satellite and cable broadcasting 15, 17
scanners 18, 19
SCONUL 28
SDI service 22
self-service photocopiers 24
service contract 19
short books 12
short loan collection 25
short stories 12
site licence initiative 16, 18
slides 13, 15, 21
Society of Archivists 28
sound recordings 6
    incidental inclusion 8
    performance 10, 24
    term of protection 6
staff training 25
statutory enquiry 11
statutory material 12
stock copying 9, 10, 22, 25
students 22
study packs 14, 25
subscription agents 21
substantial part 7, 19
subtitled copies 11
sui generis right 18

tables 6
tape levy 17
telephone directory 18
television *see* off-air recording
term of protection *see* duration of term
textbooks 27
theses 25

time-shifting 11
translating *see* adaptation right
translations 25
transmission 7
transparencies 13
typographical arrangements 6

UNESCO 6
unfair contract 24
unknown authorship 23
unpublished works 10, 24, 25
user education 25

videos 6, 23, 25; *see also* films
  case law 27
  incidental inclusion 8, 9
visually impaired 22

whole works 26
work books 21
World Wide Web 20

Yellow Pages 13